# *If* I Had a
# Water Buffalo

# *If* I Had a
# Water Buffalo

## EMPOWERING OTHERS
## THROUGH SUSTAINABLE LENDING

Marilyn A. Fitzgerald, Ph.D.

# *If* I Had a Water Buffalo
## Empowering Others Through Sustainable Lending

ISBN 978-1-61448-528-5 paperback
ISBN 978-1-61448-529-2 eBook
Library of Congress Control Number: 2013930347

Morgan James Publishing
The Entrepreneurial Publisher
5 Penn Plaza, 23rd Floor
New York City, New York 10001
(212) 655-5470 office • (516) 908-4496 fax
www.MorganJamesPublishing.com

**Cover Design by:**
Rachel Lopez
www.r2cdesign.com

In an effort to support local communities, raise awareness and funds, Morgan James Publishing donates a percentage of all book sales for the life of each book to Habitat for Humanity Peninsula and Greater Williamsburg.

 Get involved today, visit
www.MorganJamesBuilds.com.

 **Habitat**
for Humanity®
Peninsula and
Greater Williamsburg
Building Partner

As a strong and enduring proponent for personal sustainability through empowerment, Dr. Fitzgerald donates a percentage of her book sales proceeds to various organizations promoting microfinance and social business initiatives.

 www.mafitzgerald.com
marilyn@mafitgerald.com
www.facebook.com/fitzgeraldma
www.twitter.com/fitzgeraldma

*"Go to the people. Live with them, learn from them, love them. Start with what they know, build with what they have. But with the best leaders, the work is done, the task accomplished, the people will say, 'We have done this ourselves.'"*

LAO-TZU 600 BC

Dr. Fitzgerald's company, **Common Ground Solutions, LLC** (CGS), which provides consulting and publication services focused on sustainability, conflict resolution, and project management, has adopted the logo of a child's hand to represent the core philosophy of its mission of providing a Hand Up rather than a Handout.

The hand contains the following critical words describing the methods and outcomes of projects that CGS builds and endorses.

We provide *Opportunity* that leads toward *Prosperity*, utilizing the methodologies of *Microfinance* and *Social Business*; our projects are *Sustainable* and *Thrive* while respecting the *Voice, Choice* and *Dignity* of all.

# CONTENTS

## Part I: Led by the Heart;
## Doing Without Understanding     1

## Part II: From the Field
## to The Classroom and Back Again     67

## Part III:
## Lessons Learned, Lessons Shared   107

# FOREWORD

## by PROFESSOR MUHAMMAD YUNUS
### 2006 Nobel Peace Laureate

Marilyn Fitzgerald has written a warm and personal book about her experience in developing sustainable social programs that will pay for themselves while meeting important social needs. This book identifies the power of microfinance systems and social business to eliminate world poverty and liberate both the beneficiaries and the donors by decreasing the potential chronic dependency, often induced by well-intentioned charitable donors.

The simple stories, as told by Marilyn Fitzgerald from the perspective of a donor, volunteer and finally, a researcher, are derived from her personal experiences in the field. The lessons she shares with us are of value as well as pragmatic, as she has traveled a path that brought her to deeply understand the need for sustainable projects. The book illustrates nicely that microfinance does not gloss over its challenges, but demonstrates how poor can prudently use it as a tool to take on the root causes of poverty and lead to the awareness that charitable giving sometimes can become an endless trap, which in the end, will not produce the intended impact of helping others, and in fact, may cause harm by creating a dependency.

Through her profession as a psychologist, she clearly holds the human dignity of all in high regard. Microcredit organizations need to be ever vigilant for opportunities to create a culture of dignity rather than dependency and this book shows how to make it happen.

This is an insightful and practical resource forged from the vast experience of the author who challenges each of us to invest in systems that are effective and efficient.

I hope this book will add wisdom to all those who have joined the revolution of creating a poverty-free world.

Professor Muhammad Yunus
Nobel Peace Laureate'2006
Founder, Grameen Bank

# ACKNOWLEDGMENTS

It is humbling to think of the number of people who have helped and supported my travel on this journey of learning, understanding, and experience, culminating in some important life lessons. It would have been impossible to have these incredible experiences helping to shape my thinking and behavior without the hard work and dedication of many others.

My teachers in the field were people of wisdom and courage who shared knowledge, hope, and dreams for the future. Though scarce, they even shared food and water. Living in extreme poverty did not rob them of compassion, love, or big hearts; they shared shelter, were protective, and comforting in places unfamiliar to me. It was a privilege and honor to spend time in their villages; they captured a place in my heart and I am forever the beneficiary of their teaching, help, and support.

Critical to my learning process were the program managers in the field. Their genuine concern for the recipients often kept them brutally honest regarding the effectiveness or sustainability of programs in their charge. The candid sharing of their experiences in the field was essential to my overall understanding.

The members of my Rotary Club in Traverse City, Michigan, and District 6290 often had exactly the right words at the right time. My fellow Rotarians were encouraging; reminding me that I was not just one person. I am part of a wonderful international service organization and we are in this together. To my most special Rotary mentors I say, "If I have seen a little further it is by standing on the shoulders of Giants." You are Giants!

For his unwavering support, encouragement, and friendship, I am deeply grateful to Alan F. Olson. If not for his advance financial funding, the ideas percolating in my mind may never have made it to the publication of this book. Alan believed in this message from the beginning. He supported it and I am happy to call him my friend.

Casting his professional writing skills toward this book, Dr. Stephen G. Tolley edited the manuscript multiple times. I am forever grateful for his uncommon patience as he took the time to help me organize my thoughts and then find my voice to tell the story in my own words. I am thankful for our eternal friendship.

Most recently, Michael J. Smith has provided my homeland security. He has ensured that I had a roof over my head, food in my tummy, and numerous rides to the airport on my trips to the field and delivered welcome-home hugs upon my return. He has risen above my countless hours of writing, at the end of the day, taken me sailing, and made me laugh. I am very appreciative.

My two daughters, Debbie and Jenny, have been encouraging of this particular project and unconditional in their love and lifelong support. I have learned many of my life lessons witnessing the courage and joy in which they live their lives. I am proud, grateful, and privileged to be their mom. These two exceptional women have brought to our family two extraordinary grandchildren and they are delightful! Ryan is in college, smart and handsome. He inspires me with his voracious curiosity and with never-ending questions about the research, he makes me stretch. Amaya is in elementary school and she too is smart, cute, and overflowing with personality. She inspires me with her endless energy and challenging questions on why it takes so long to write just one book! Watching my daughters and grandchildren move through their lives with compassion toward humankind brings me great comfort knowing the future is in good hands.

A sincere thank you to colleagues, and special friends that have contributed along my life path of learning, you have enriched my life, and are forever etched in my heart.

## A SPECIAL THANK YOU TO
### ROTARY INTERNATIONAL

For the past nineteen years it has been my privilege to be a proud member of Rotary International in the Rotary Club of Traverse City, Michigan, District 6290. Rotary International and the Rotary Foundation have provided me life-changing opportunities that would not have possible if not for my membership and I am forever grateful.

The projects incorporated in the dissertation research were not related to Rotary due to potential conflict of interest. However, it has been my honor to be involved in numerous community and international projects. Rotary International have endorsed the value of bringing together business and professional leaders to encourage Service Above Self, promote high ethical standards in all vocations, and build goodwill and peace in the world.

# PROLOGUE

*"It is better to light one small candle
than to curse the darkness."*

ELEANOR ROOSEVELT

Regardless of our personal journeys, areas of interest, endeavors, or issues we undertake in life, one of the outcomes is often an assembly of lessons learned, some are easily learned while others are often hard fought and finally learned the hard way. The distinctive lessons for each of us will be very specific, while others are more generalized, making them applicable to much of life—personal, family, business, school, or community. Such are the lessons that I share in this book. Garnered from humanitarian-aid efforts impacting poverty-stricken villages and homes in Central America, Eastern Europe, Indonesia, and Bangladesh as well as the knowledge acquired in a university classroom, these lessons have near universal applicability, transcending their roots in humanitarian aid.

My journey into the world of humanitarian-aid projects began with my increasing awareness of the dire plight of so many people in the world and because of an ever-present, ever-growing conflict within me: how could I live in such comfort while so many others struggled with abject poverty? Witnessing poverty firsthand, seeing the desperate looks in mothers' eyes during my first trip to Indonesia, forever etched these gaping needs into my heart. Humanitarian-aid projects—seeking methods that would enable others to gain pride, dignity, and self-sufficiency—has become my passion, fueled by a never-ending internal conflict that compels me to take action.

The inner conflict never escapes me and is only heightened when I walk through the doors of my home. I do not sleep on a dirt floor. The food I eat sits in cupboards after I unload groceries bought at clean, brightly lit stores. Those that I visited abroad have no cupboards or food. I do not hike to the river to bathe or to do the family laundry. I don't carry a five-gallon jug of drinking water on my head for hours each day. The fact that I can control the temperature of the room, turn on and off lights with a flip of a switch, and take a hot shower with clean water is unimaginable to many people I have visited in impoverished countries. My car can transport me anytime I wish to go; there is no need to wait for the "chicken bus" to take me to the market. Opportunity for education has always been within my reach. Never have members of my family been faced with the requirement to flee for safety, taking only the possessions they could carry. I have never rocked my children to sleep while they cried from hunger. I have always had the right and ability to openly speak my opinion, and my nation's constitution declares that I have the right to pursue my own happiness. The litany of my privileges and good fortune, compared to the lack thereof of hundreds of millions of people around the world, plays and replays in my mind. And this gave birth to my deep desire, need, and responsibility to share my time, talent, and treasures with those in need. And that, in turn, gave birth to lessons learned—lessons that will serve so many walks in life—now shared through the writing of this book.

*If I Had a Water Buffalo* is divided into three parts:

Part I, "Led by the Heart: Doing Without Understanding," describes a series of humanitarian-aid efforts I had the privilege of being involved in. Working with service club organizations, volunteers, poverty-stricken families, and caring citizens, I was a small part of the overall efforts, but those efforts became a very big part of me. Although we had the best intentions, often our efforts were not well thought out and frequently they contained trappings that would forever shackle the beneficiaries to the donors and create dependency on others. Luck was on our side, and, in the short-term, we were successful.

Each lesson learned was valuable and had its place in the larger picture, but I could not yet fully see just how the pieces fit together.

Part II, "From the Field to the Classroom and Back Again," describes an unexpected turn in my journey, brought about by a professor's question: "Do you think the provision of resources in the form of humanitarian-aid projects ever causes conflict for the people you are trying to help?" He recited an eye-opening story about how a new water system, supplied by the good intentions of a service organization, caused great conflict and forever changed the social dynamic of an impoverished community.

I needed and wanted to learn more. I wanted to learn about preventing and resolving conflict that might arise during the course of a humanitarian-aid project, how best to guide the efforts, and how to make every humanitarian-aid dollar count. So many times I had heard that peace in the world is not possible until the issue of poverty is alleviated; in heartfelt efforts to remedy poverty, how could we potentially be increasing conflict? In the endless search for answers, I entered an academic program focused on conflict analysis and resolution to further expand my global perspective.

My studies at the university offered exposure to additional project tools, resources, and an incredible opportunity to interface with many international students. Each student was seeking to better understand the dynamics of conflict and how best to resolve it—conflict that impacted their lives, their communities, and their nations. The final hurdle in the academic pursuit was planning for and conducting research as part of the dissertation process. It was this research that took me back to the field, but in a different and constrained role—the role of an objective observer rather than a passionate doer.

Part III, "Lessons Learned, Lessons Shared," incorporates five fundamental outcomes from my journey to date. These outcomes, presented as lessons shared, were derived from the field of humanitarian aid but are equally applicable to almost every endeavor one might take in life. *Sustainability* incorporates more than the bottom line and integrates social and economic well-being. *Relationship building* is the tool that changes a group of individuals into a collective force. *Integrative negotiation* provides the means to complement one another in the pursuit of objectives, rather than compete. It offers an opportunity for all stakeholders to engage in a win-win rather than win-lose outcome. *Project management* is an organized means to move from idea/concept to project completion and evaluation while constantly remaining focused on meeting the objectives of the project. Finally, the *synchronicity of microfinance and social business* is incorporated to complete (for now) the lessons shared. Microfinance provides small amounts of funding to entrepreneurs who live in poverty and do not have access to traditional systems of borrowing money, due to lack of a credit history or collateral. In the past, these individuals often fell prey to unscrupulous lenders that charged high interest rates that would forever lock the borrower in debt to the lender. Social business is a natural extension of microfinance. As first defined by Professor Muhammad Yunus, microfinance integrates an organization's development and success in addressing a social objective in a manner that meets criteria for sustainability.

However, the real power of the five lessons shared comes from weaving them together!

May these lessons shared be used as tools that permit your projects to progress more smoothly, produce outcomes equal to expectations, and be put forth in a manner that bears witness to the individuals and families gripped by poverty today, but searching for a better tomorrow.

# PART I

## LED BY THE HEART; DOING WITHOUT UNDERSTANDING

*"Unless you're willing to have a go, fail miserably, and have another go, success won't happen."*

PHILLIP ADAMS

*"Courage doesn't always roar. Sometimes courage is the quiet voice at the end of the day saying, "I will try again tomorrow."*

MARY ANNE RADAMACHER

# Introduction

Life and life's lessons are not always straightforward. What I thought was simply another trip to an Indonesian village, as part of an all-out effort to fund the education of every child in the village, turned out be the first step in my journey to truly understanding and passionately believing in sustainable giving—thanks to a poor rice farmer and his need for a water buffalo. The first step of this wonderful, winding, heart-tugging, and enlightening journey was launched with his simple question: "Does she want to help?"

Perhaps if this had been my first trip to that village, my reaction to the farmer's question might have been different. But things happen for a reason and, as far as the farmer was concerned, all my efforts to date had not provided the help that he needed—help that would promote sustainability. On that hot, humid day, standing by the rice field, I don't know if the farmer was asking for sustainability as he spoke to me through the interpreter, and I certainly wasn't thinking in terms of sustainable giving as I listened.

"Does she want to help?" asked Nyoman, as he momentarily paused from his backbreaking labor of tilling the rice fields with his wooden hoe to approach the interpreter.

"Of course," was my answer.

Nyoman was prepared for the follow-up: If I wanted to help, he needed a water buffalo. I should provide him with a water buffalo to plow the rice fields and then he would be able to pay the tuition to send his children to school. Then Nyoman, his wife, and his children would no longer be dependent on far-away donors.

I was the personification of that donor process as I stood with Nyoman that day. I had thought that we—the donors from afar—were meeting the educational needs of the village; I'd thought we were doing a good thing from the very start. And then I thought back to the beginning and how the cyclic process of annually funding the educational needs of the village had led to this day.

*"Education is the most powerful weapon which you
can use to change the world."*

NELSON MANDELA

CHAPTER ONE

# FOCUSING ON EDUCATION AND NUTRITION

## IN THE BEGINNING

Having completed a seemingly successful effort to fund, build, and supply a new blood bank in Bali, Indonesia, those that I represented, worked with, and other donors turned our attention to the children. Our local service club formed partnerships with other service clubs, nonprofit, and non-governmental organizations (NGOs) located in developing countries for the purpose of providing resources for humanitarian projects. The resources of all parties consisted of time, treasure, and talent.

The government of Indonesia provides free education for all children through the elementary grade levels, but the families must purchase the uniforms and school supplies. Tragically, thousands of families living in abject poverty in rural Indonesia cannot afford to send their children to school. Many of the children begin working in the rice fields as soon as they are physically capable, providing labor to help feed their families. *The Annual United Nations Report: The Status of the World's Children* (2000) confirmed that the children of Indonesia are living in the poorest economic conditions of all the children in Asia. The document further reported that 33,000 of those children are living in extreme poverty with limited access to adequate nutrition, safe drinking water, medical care, and education. Thousands die prematurely of preventable causes. The surviving children are subject to conditions that, if left unchanged, will shape the destiny of future generations to repeat the same cycle of poverty.

In 2009, the United Nations reported that on a daily basis, there were approximately 24,000 preventable deaths worldwide—primarily children—due to a lack of proper nutrition, access to clean drinking water, and a lack of medical services. Those numbers are mind-boggling! That means 24,000 preventable deaths yesterday, today, and tomorrow: the days, months, and years behind and ahead of us. It is almost impossible to imagine or to process in our minds and hearts, even though we read the numbers and have seen the pictures of mothers holding their starving, dying babies. We even see these children in television commercials pleading for help and intervention from early-childhood preventable death. Many of us do respond to their plea for help by donating money.

During my visits to rural impoverished villages in developing countries, the greetings often included mothers eagerly, carefully, and lovingly handing me their infants and children to hold. Sometimes, they stood in line to have their child held for just a few minutes as we exchanged glances of sympathy and concern for the well-being of these children. While I loved to hold the children, each time I did so it was a vivid reminder of the differences in our worlds. These children had bloated tummies, were mostly naked, and showed clear evidence of malnutrition. For the mothers, the simple gesture of their children being held by an outsider, perhaps with access to resources—one who might seek to bring about a change—was a gesture of hope. Hope that a change would come to their world and that their children would have opportunities they did not.

These visits left me both heartsick and determined to find a way to make a difference. Many service clubs and various NGOs agree that education and proper nutrition provide children a clear path out of impoverished conditions.

## FINDING A WAY

The Children's Educational Sponsorship Program in Indonesia was established to open the door to education and address the nutritional needs of children whose parents were unable to afford the cost of sending them to school. Just $60 a year provides one child a school uniform, shoes, books and supplies, a cup of rice a day, meat twice a week, and a daily nutritional supplement.

When I was first drawn to this program, it seemed reasonable that our partner service clubs would start with a small number of children. We agreed that twenty would be the number and that those children would come from one of the rural impoverished villages. The strategy and math seemed simple. To do what we had committed to would require raising $1,200 annually. If successful, we would consider raising funds for multiple years of education. The service clubs in the United States were separated from our partner service clubs in Indonesia by 12,000 miles but were joined by a common goal, and through their respective meetings, they overwhelmingly endorsed our goal. Generosity flowed from club members and residents of the communities once the story began to circulate about the plight and despair of the children living in extreme poverty in rural Indonesia.

The money needed was not only raised quickly, but the original goal was exceeded. Raising more money than originally intended was exciting. However, the $8,000 we raised came with questions: Was it best to increase the number of children to attend school for one year or should we fund fewer children for multiple years? What was the best formula to disburse the donations to ensure that we complied with the donors' intention regarding the funding of the children's education?

To answer these questions and others, it was decided that without using any of the education donations, I would visit the village again to assist in developing, along with our local partners, the necessary mechanisms and systems that would address the most efficient and effective method of disbursing the donated funds. It was important to all that the donors' money have the best possible impact for the children.

The journey to remote areas of Indonesia is not easy. To reach the final destination, requires traveling more than 12,000 miles by air, followed by hours spent in the heat and humidity, bouncing along the bumpy, dusty, or muddy roads, often in a vehicle that seems incapable of completing the trip. When the roads give way to the rain forest, we hike.

As usual, upon arriving in Indonesia, I met up with Freddy—my friend, interpreter, and partner in these endeavors. Freddy knew the language, the culture, and the people, and possessed an incredible passion to improve the lives of his less fortunate fellow Indonesians. Freddy was a humanitarian; his compassion was contagious and others willingly followed his lead. As we hiked toward the village, Freddy and I felt a degree of satisfaction anticipating that twenty children would soon have the opportunity to attend school. We imagined their excitement and joy. But this hope was quickly dwarfed by the starkness and desperation we saw upon our arrival at the village. In the face of the hundreds desperately wanting to attend school but unable to afford the annual $60 fee, our plans to educate twenty paled when compared to the obvious need.

The silent pleas of the children not selected and their parents began to consume me. Yes, we had $8,000, but there was neither a long-term plan nor assurance that there would be future financial support from the donors. Members of Freddy's service club sat, sipped tea, and shared in goodwill and fellowship as we collectively tried to construct a plan for the best use of the funds we had. But in the pit of my stomach I knew this was not enough money and I could not walk away feeling good about our original goal. We needed to do more!

### From 20 to 500 Students: The Hole Gets Deeper!

Before the sun set on our first day in the village, Freddy and I decided that my local service club and community in a distant land would find a way to raise the necessary funds to send 500 children to school for one year. The village elders expressed their gratitude and joy as Freddy made the announcement, but we quickly figured that we needed a *lot* more money. The $8,000 was almost insignificant compared to the new level of commitment. As the realization sank in, I had a similar sinking feeling in my stomach—as the annual fundraising goal shot from $1,200 to $30,000.

> Setting goals and making budget decisions on an emotional, gut level is not the smartest thing to do ...

Setting goals and making budget decisions on an emotional, gut level is not the smartest thing to do, especially while still in the field, yet that was what we had done. And I found myself firmly ensconced in the dreaded yet familiar land of "project creep" or "mission expansion" hanging without a strategy or a clue about how to achieve the goal. Yet I was determined that collectively we could and would make it happen.

When I returned home, the reality of the situation haunted my daily life. What would happen to these children next year? Would this be enough education to teach them to read and write? Every child in the world is entitled to more than one year of education; we needed to make it happen! Gandhi's words, "Be the change," became my mantra. But what action could I take? With no long-term strategy and increasing anxiety, my heart carried me into another personal commitment. I made a unilateral decision to raise educational sponsorships for these 500 children for not one, but for three consecutive years of schooling.

Could we hold the interest of donors for three consecutive years and collect $30,000 annually? I spent many sleepless nights wondering, hoping, and praying to find the right words to inspire others to keep making donations. How could/would I help the donors understand their impact and significance to the families and children in this remote, rural, impoverished community thousands of miles away—people the donors would probably never meet? Would the donors listen to their stories with their hearts? Feelings of fear and panic seemed ever present when I thought about the future I was carving for myself and fellow club members. As I attempted to push my feelings aside, imagining I was moving forward, in reality, I was digging the donors and myself deeper and deeper into an unrealistic commitment. It was so easy to do as I remembered the look of excitement in the eyes of the children who were lucky enough to be selected by the elders of the village to receive an education; I just kept imagining more and more happy faces.

## DELIVERING THE MESSAGE

After each visit to Indonesia, I would sequester myself for several days, organizing the photos of children and my notes in order to report back to the service clubs and other patrons who were donating funds for the educational sponsorships. I wanted them to know that their money was making a difference. I wanted them to feel the same spirit of gratitude from the beneficiaries that I was so fortunate to experience firsthand. How the message was received directly impacted the possibility of any long-term commitment.

Since this was in pre-digital camera days, I had hundreds of pictures of children, the village, and the broken-down classrooms to develop at the local drugstore and then sort through. Carefully I selected images that would help me best tell the story and attract additional donors. Frequently, the photos I found most rewarding were those that showed children in their new uniforms receiving books and school supplies, always with big smiles on their faces. I also selected pictures of specific groups of children being supported by individuals, businesses, and service clubs, so donors would see progress—the physical growth of familiar children—hoping they would feel like part of something good and meaningful.

I made presentations to numerous service groups as well as to good-hearted friends, family, and neighbors; sharing with them the stories of the many village residents living in poverty and their hopes and dreams of education for their children. It seemed like such a big responsibility to convey the village life in a way that was informative and that also inspired the donors to keep giving. I was the voice for those who could not be present to tell their own stories.

After hearing my presentations, many of these compassionate people contributed to the educational fundraising effort. I felt enormous relief and deep gratitude for the people in my home community, the region, and for the international foundation that often matched the locally raised funds. Through individual donations and grants, we finally generated enough money—$30,000—to send 500 children to school for one year!

Believing these children needed an advocate I became determined to be their voice. And through my voice, along with the photos and presentations, the donors were able to see their dollars transformed into the smiling faces of children.

Not only was education being provided for yet another year through the sponsorship program, but undernourished children were receiving a cup of rice a day, a small portion of meat twice a week, and a daily nutritional supplement—a start to preventing malnutrition or, worse, early preventable death. The donors' money was doing exactly what they intended.

> What if the dreaded donor fatigue set in and the children's needs were not met?

The donors were happy and the children were happy, yet I was still not at peace.

How long could we hold the donors' interest? What if the dreaded *donor fatigue* set in and the children's needs were not met? I tried to dismiss these thoughts, assuring myself that I'd just keep moving forward ... digging the hole a little deeper. But the hole was also providing for the immediate needs of the children, and it was wonderful to see!

### SEEING DOLLARS TURN INTO SMILES

Each time we visited the village this scene was repeated: Hundreds of bare feet would scamper through the rutty brown-dirt streets toward my cohorts and we would be greeted with heartwarming hugs and smiles. The air sparkled with anticipation and appreciation. As we, once again, celebrated that the money had arrived, there were big smiles and tears of gratitude and joy from the families and children—followed by my own tears of happiness and pride. My work felt important and my heart was filled with gratitude for the donors and for this life-changing experience that so enriched me, increasing my appreciation for the world.

## The Children and the School

The children began their education by developing basic literacy skills: identifying numbers and letters, learning to write, and finally, learning to read—opening a whole new world of possibility to them through books. Reading and writing were skills that their parents and grandparents had never acquired, but the adults were eager for their children to learn in the hope that they and future generations would have a better life.

The school was not a wonderful or comfortable place, but I loved spending time with the children there. The building, a dilapidated, falling-down structure, did not resemble the typical schoolrooms in the U.S. There were no brightly decorated bulletin boards, freshly painted walls, clean floors, library, computer labs, or cafeteria and gym. Instead, there was one room, with many children gathered around a broken-down, water-damaged, splintering table. Many children shared a bench or just stood next to the table for their lessons. The school was built with donated money from foreign charities, with no consideration for the cost of upkeep. The residents of the village tried to maintain the structure, but they had no money for improvements or repair after the annual monsoon storms. The ceiling consisted of large pieces of plywood with gaping holes, permitting all of nature's elements to come streaming into the room. The walls were mildewed and moldy. The classroom was always dark because there was no electricity; so to read from their tattered books, the children would often sit in a line on the ground outside the classroom where sunlight made it easier to see the print. The books were shared and they stayed at school—never to be borrowed or taken home. Classroom supplies were scarce and treasured. Each student was given a piece of paper, which was meant to last for the week, and a pencil. I made a mental note to bring pencil sharpeners on my next visit, as I watched the teacher sharpen a stack of pencils with a dull knife. Despite the conditions, both students and teachers seemed grateful for the experience.

In addition to the dearth of supplies, there were no sanitation facilities at the school—a fact I learned the hard way. After a long drive to the village, then a hike up a footpath to reach the school—drinking water throughout the four-hour trip—I asked for a restroom. In response, I was led to the dense forest behind the building. After that particular experience, with children peeking from behind trees and giggling, I learned to pace my consumption of water before visiting the school.

The best part about visiting the school was the energy of the children! They seemed so happy, polite, well-behaved, and anxious to demonstrate their new knowledge to visitors. The children would learn just enough English to greet me, which always put a huge smile on my face. I learned just enough Indonesian to respond, "*Selamat siang! Nama saya Marilyn.*"

(Good afternoon! My name is Marilyn.)—which made them giggle, as my carefully thought-out and pronounced Indonesian syllables missed the mark considerably.

In the classroom, the children would proudly, and sometimes shyly, walk forward to the worn-out chalkboard. Shiny with age and use, the board was also weathered from exposure to the rain, sun, and heat coming through the roof and ceiling. Standing before the board, the teacher would give the child who came forward a problem to solve along with a small piece of chalk, which was held in their little hand as if it were a precious piece of gold. Total silence filled the room as the child wrote his or her answer on the board. The classroom had one abacus, and sometimes another child would jump over to it and try to race the child at the chalkboard to the solution. When the teacher confirmed that the answer given by the student at the board was correct, the entire class erupted with a cheer. Watching the children blossom through education, my spirit soared. I was exactly where I was meant to be.

> The school was built with donated money from foreign charities, with no consideration for the cost of upkeep.

The children attending school appeared physically better, stronger, and brighter-eyed than those who could not. Their clean, well-fitted uniforms included one pair of shoes—for some, the only pair they had ever owned. It was not uncommon to see the children running to and from school barefoot, carrying their shoes. The shoes were actually on their feet only during school hours. I was never sure if this was because they were trying to save their shoes solely for the specific purpose of attending school or if they were so accustomed to going barefoot it was more comfortable.

One of the teachers shared with me that often the biggest incentive for the children to attend school was the access to daily food. On days that they did not attend school, there was often very little or even no food at home, which meant that they might not have anything to eat until the next school day. This was doubly heartbreaking because there were families with four or five children, and we were only sponsoring one or two of them in the education program. What were the other children in the family eating?

## What About the Ones Left Behind?

It was heart wrenching to walk through the village on the way to the school and see the children not attending. These children desperately wanted to go to school too, but like so many others, their parents could not afford the annual $60 fee. It did not take long for me to convince myself that our goal must be for every child in that village to be enrolled in school. It was more than a goal; it was a matter of necessity. It was impossible for me to think objectively. My heart ruled me. Just think: What would this village be like if every child went to school, if every child received enough nutrition to ensure that his or her brain could grow and develop? How hard could it be to make this happen? After all, this was just one small village.

Being optimistic, but somewhat naïve, I thought that the majority of the children were already in school. My guesstimate was that about a hundred or so children were not. With conviction, I determined that it was only right that these children also have an education. Unfortunately, the conviction was not accompanied by any long-term plan or strategy. The new goal was emotionally driven.

Freddy and I met with the village elders to make the

announcement: Every child in the village would attend school. They were overjoyed. Then we learned the true number of children involved. It was not the 100 that I had figured but rather several hundred. The elders confirmed there were about 1,200 children living in this village. We were now funding 500 and had offered a passionate, emotion-driven promise to fund 700 more. Our work was cut out for the service clubs, the donors, Freddy, and me.

## A PROMISE FOR 1,200 CHILDREN

On the return trip to the States, I again did the math. The magic number was $72,000—the amount needed to fund all 1,200 children to attend school for one year. Keeping in mind the challenge of raising the initial $30,000 for the 500 children, I was not confident that there would be the public will or the resources to raise $72,000. This was such a huge amount, and it would only fund the children to attend school for one year of education. But, the alternative of denying some children an education was unthinkable. We just had to make it happen.

Once again, I chose pictures for my presentations and set about meeting with many of the donors, some of the service clubs involved, and other supporters of the program. However, unlike after the previous trips, I did not immediately share with them the new goal. I could not quite speak the words just yet. The people I met with were anxious to hear the success stories and see the new pictures. Congratulatory comments flowed freely for all of our efforts in sending 500 children to school. The donors were happy and so were those village children and their parents, but a storm cloud of uncertainty was brewing inside me.

## TAKING PAUSE

As days passed, the storm cloud expanded. At home, when my mind was idle, the faces of the children left behind in the villages, laboring in the rice fields, haunted me. They would watch me walk through the village with empty, sad eyes. What impact would it have on the culture of a village when only some children were sponsored for school? I daydreamed solutions, weighed down by an ever-present sense of responsibility. Several times I had gone to their village with the intention of helping—yet they took care of me. They shared their limited food and they opened their hearts and lives to me. Some of them told me their dreams; they looked at me with hope.

Thirty-three thousand Indonesian children are without basic education. What if all of this was a futile effort? Would it even matter if I convinced everyone I knew to support a child for a year of education? In the bigger picture, would it make a significant difference if I spent my energy giving presentations to tell the story of the children, getting donations, writing grants to educate so few, when the children of an entire nation were desperate for this basic right? Was it realistic to think we could really help? Would donor fatigue keep us short of our goal? Perhaps we might just rest for a while on the goodwill achieved, rather than dig the hole deeper with grander goals. What was I thinking when I raised the goal to $72,000 and announced it to the village elders?

Oh, that's right. I wasn't thinking at all; I was just feeling raw emotion. Seeing the poor, desperate, hungry children wanting to go to school and believing that they represented the hope and future of the community, it had seemed the only promise worth making; it had felt so achievable at that moment. Now, it felt so scary and maybe even beyond our grasp.

## FACING THE GIANT

I fought fear with determination. I made the leap and began consulting with some of the donors. We agreed the new annual goal of $72,000 would be a challenge but still worth pursuing, and at the end of the day, we would work with the funds we were able to accumulate. As we discussed the budget, I could not help but wonder if the donors understood the path we were paving for ourselves. Unvoiced were the obvious questions: If we are successful this year, then what about next year? If we commit to this, who will tell the elders if we cannot make our goal? How long can we keep this fundraising up; are we making a long-term commitment?

It was time for another trip to the village.

Each visit was a mixed blessing. I was so happy to see the familiar families, but in the shadows of their thoughts were looming concerns: how long would the donors be willing to support this program? I shared their concerns and found myself always searching for the right words. Words that would offer comfort and assurance to the villagers that some of their children would be educated for another year, and words that would convince the donors of the importance of this program. But those unvoiced questions were an ever-present elephant in the room that was not being acknowledged by the donors, the beneficiaries, or most of all, me.

## GROWING DEPENDENCY

With few exceptions, the villagers were dependent upon external support—donors—to fund the education of their children. But funding one-year cycles was like planting annual flowers. Beautiful to look at for a season, but you start all over again next spring. Surely there must be a better way, and, as I would come to learn, there is.

It was on this visit that Nyoman, the rice farmer, showed me that better way. In doing so, he rescued his community and me from the hole of dependency that had been created. It all started with his need for a water buffalo.

## LESSONS LEARNED

1. **We needed an exit strategy.**

   Looking back, I don't remember any of the donors asking me what the long-term plan was for this project or if we had an exit strategy in the future. Even without these two vital components, they kept contributing money to a project that they were convinced was worthy. I was so very grateful for their generous hearts.

2. **Feeling good is fine, as long as it is not a dangerous elixir.**

   There was tremendous personal satisfaction in the effort to help others, and we believed *we were making a positive difference in the world.* There I was, successfully influencing people to contribute funds in order to send impoverished children to school, believing our hard work changed lives, maybe even saved lives; I felt empowered! This activity gave me a surge of adrenaline and the good feelings were indescribable, but regrettably it turned out to be a dangerous elixir for me and the people I was trying to help.

3. **We created dependency.**

   Dependency, through annual fundraising, had a grip on the donors, the beneficiaries, and me. Ultimately, it was causing harm rather than helping. What had become the new reality had seemed impossible because when we started, the intentions of all were so good.

*"Courage is what it takes to stand up and speak;
courage is also what it takes to sit down and listen."*

NELSON MANDELA

---

CHAPTER TWO

# FUNDING A WATER BUFFALO

## DOES SHE REALLY WANT TO HELP?

After spending yet another year raising funds (with the occasional good-natured arm twisting of the donors) for the specific purpose of paying tuition for children to attend school, I found myself once again back in Indonesia standing on the edge of a rice field. Although this was my fourth trip, it turned out to be the first step in a very different journey: truly understanding the importance of sustainable giving.

Accompanying me was Freddy and another interpreter. We were sifting through mounds of paperwork, searching for names of children and trying to identify whether or not a specific child was on the list eligible for educational sponsorship. It was then when Nyoman approached Freddy and asked, "Does she really want to help?"

It was much later when I would come to understand how very important Nyoman's question was and the impact it would have on my approach to charitable giving. That singular question would send me on a path to examine the motive, method, and ultimately the impact of the "help" that so many others and myself were providing.

"Yes, of course I want to help!" I told Freddy to tell Nyoman. Then I gave his question a bit more thought. It seemed odd that this rice farmer would question my sincere desire to help. To me, the effort and good intentions to help were obvious—just by our presence in his village.

Freddy assured Nyoman that yes, this lady—representing the citizens of her hometown in Northern Michigan and her service organization—wanted to help educate the impoverished children in his village. As Freddy explained that money was collected for the village children so they would have the opportunity to attend school, he smiled at Nyoman and, with enthusiasm, pointed to the children, to the shabby school building, and to both of us. He exuded pride, sincerity, and a good deal of animation, as he appeared to be describing the effort involved in our desire to help.

Nyoman listened but never changed the expression on his face. When Freddy finished, he replied, "If you really want to help, I need a water buffalo."

I was sure something had been mixed up in the translation; so I asked Freddy to ask the rice farmer to repeat his question.

"Do you really want to help us?" was Nyoman's response.

Again, I nodded affirmatively to both Freddy and the rice farmer. "Yes, we do want to help pay for the education of children." I hoped this would clarify the donors' intention.

"If you really want to help, I need a water buffalo," repeated Nyoman.

Perplexed, I returned to my clipboard and the children who had begun to surround us, leaving it to Freddy to explain that we do not fund water buffalos, just education for children. But, a few minutes later, prompted by a mild curiosity, I asked Nyoman with Freddy's help, "Why do you want a water buffalo?"

Turning toward the beautiful, terraced rice field and leaning against his primitive, handmade hoe, Nyoman began to explain: "The land is leased and rice crop harvested by hand, which is a slow, tedious process. If I had a water buffalo (which apparently equated to owning a John Deere tractor to him), I would be able to harvest the rice field three times a year, tripling the capacity of the rice field and my income."

"What would you do with the additional income?" we asked.

Nyoman gestured to my clipboard and said that the names of three of his children were listed there. His voice slowed as he told Freddy that if he had the additional income, he could afford to send his own children to school and they would not be on our list.

I heard a loud click inside me. "How much does a water buffalo cost?" we asked him.

Nyoman didn't know for sure, but after more discussion between Freddy and Nyoman—what sounded like an Indonesian negotiation—they seemed to agree a water buffalo could be purchased in a neighboring village for about $250.

The chat ended with us assuring Nyoman we would give his idea some thought, and we turned our attention back to the task at hand—confirming the names of children on our extensive lists. Nothing more was discussed about the purchase of a water buffalo before Freddy and I departed from the village. Our work was completed for one more year; all the children's names were verified on the list. It was time to head home and begin the fundraising cycle once again.

Homeward bound on a comfortable plane was a special time for me to relax and think about the journey: what it meant to the donors, the children, the village, and to me. It was gratifying to think of the hopeful and thankful faces of the children and their mothers. Recalling the extraordinary people living in the village, experiencing their generous hospitality, seeing how much the children had grown since the last visit, and feeling privileged to be exposed to their culture and daily routine was heartwarming. But, my mind also drifted to Nyoman and his desire for a water buffalo.

**For the first time ever my numbers would be reduced rather than snowballing upward.**

I tried to imagine the impact a water buffalo might have on his life and that of his children. Two hundred and fifty dollars seemed like so little money if it would actually provide an opportunity to lift Nyoman and his family to an economic level where he could financially support the education of his own children. Plus, there was a direct benefit if Nyoman had his water buffalo: I would reduce my annual fundraising goal. The fundraising effort was providing educational sponsorships to 1,200 children; the purchase of a water buffalo would reduce that number to 1,197. For the first time ever my numbers would be reduced rather than snowballing upward. Instead of raising $72,000 annually, the goal would be $71, 820; I was grinning on the inside as I ran the numbers; my MBA was really paying off!

How do I fund the purchase of a water buffalo? I did not want to go back to the donors and explain this, potentially diverting some of the school sponsorship money. Especially since I was not sure how long it would take Nyoman to achieve a return on the investment of the water buffalo and subsequently afford to send his own children to school. That message would be too complicated and risky for my relationship with the donors if things did not go according to plan, but I did have an idea of where to go for the money.

## All I Want for Christmas

As the holidays approached, my family asked me what I wanted for Christmas. In response, filled with energy and brimming with hope, I blurted, "I want a water buffalo!" Everybody stopped talking; they were stunned. I had never asked for livestock before; we were city people. After a moment they started making jokes, asking if I was still suffering from jet lag, or if I had remembered to take my malaria medication, and if all my shots were up-to-date before this last trip. My family has a special gene for sarcasm. When their jokes and teasing settled down, they realized I was serious. Finally we could have the conversation.

"Okay, Mom, why do you want a water buffalo?"

It was exciting to tell them about Nyoman and his family, and how the water buffalo would be equal to one of our farmers receiving a John Deere tractor. Nyoman would be much more efficient and could triple his income by harvesting his crop three times a year with the proper equipment. Currently, he could harvest his crop only once a year using his handmade hoe. Nyoman would use the additional income to pay the school fees for his children and my list of children would be reduced from 1,200 to 1,197. It was exhilarating to tell them about the prospect of helping Nyoman and his family. I hoped they would share my enthusiasm and be unable to resist my desire for a cash gift. Judging from the looks on their faces, I was not so sure.

On Christmas Day, I was handed a beautifully wrapped box with a bow; it couldn't be money because that would have been in an envelope. For a few seconds I thought the family might not have taken me seriously and I skipped past my desire for a water buffalo. When I ripped off the wrapping paper, opened the box, and pushed back the tissue paper, there it was: two hundred and fifty $1 bills! I had never seen that much cash in a box wrapped like that; I was so happy I wept—because I knew what this would mean for Nyoman.

Immediately after the holidays, I wired the money to Freddy, and he helped Nyoman purchase a water buffalo from the neighboring village. It was perfect! A handwritten fax from Freddy confirmed when the water buffalo arrived in the village. There was a Balinese Hindu ceremony to celebrate and bless Nyoman, his water buffalo, and the rice field; the whole village attended and joyfully participated. I could not stop smiling for a week.

## Luck and Good Fortune on Our Side

The next year, when Nyoman greeted our arrival at the village, he walked toward us with pride. There appeared to be a new sense of purpose and dignity; his children and wife were no longer waiting in line and dependent on my help, and they too walked confidently with him. When Nyoman first saw us, he gestured for Freddy and me to follow him into the rice field; this was not my idea of a good time. I loved *looking* at the rice fields, especially when the sun was rising or setting, but not walking in them. The terraced field had been flooded the day before and, even though Nyoman was pointing to a path to walk on, it was still ankle-deep mud. I was not barefoot like most people working in the rice fields, and it soon became obvious that my new sandals would be trashed. Leery of rice snakes, even though they were not poisonous, I didn't like seeing them when my feet were in the mud.

Reluctantly, I followed Nyoman down the path, keeping my eyes focused on the ground. When the procession stopped, I looked up, and there—right in front of me—was a water buffalo! She looked huge standing on the hillside in the shade with dried mud up to her shoulder blades. Nyoman stood next to her, proudly stroking her neck, as we both looked into her big, soft, brown eyes. He spoke lovingly, as though she was a friend.

Fighting off big flies and withering in the stifling heat, this was an incredible, heartwarming experience. There was Nyoman in his field, dressed in his sarong and straw hat, displaying an ever-widening, toothless smile, standing taller and prouder than I had ever seen him.

"*Ibu Marilyn!*" he said sincerely. He was introducing me to Mother/Madam Marilyn. He had named his water buffalo after me!

Throughout the remaining days of this visit, seeing Nyoman and Ibu Marilyn working together in the rice field fueled an ever-glowing smile within me, and I held close the thought *this is good!* This one act of donating a water buffalo seemed to change the mood of the village. Not only Nyoman, but others too, were filled with energy and hope. He was given the opportunity to support and provide for his own family as well as contribute to his village community by donating rice to those in need.

> Donating a water buffalo seemed to change the mood of the village.

We had been wrong in our earlier approach, and it took a water buffalo to show me the way. Given the right circumstances and opportunity, people can, will, and have the desire to help themselves—and, in fact, they may even have their own solutions.

## Lighting the Entrepreneurial Fire

Unbeknownst to me, watching Nyoman's success and prosperity, lit the fire of entrepreneurship and self-help in the women of the village. They began meeting to discuss what they might do similar to Nyoman. They were creatively transitioning from *dependency thinking* into the arena of *possibility thinking*. What would or could they do if they had resources available to them? What would be most valuable to them, their families, and their community? They were brainstorming ways to earn enough money to pay for the education of their children. They were growing less and less content with the system of waiting every year, wondering if someone, a foreigner, a stranger would show up in the village, and if they did, would they bring enough money for all of their children to attend school?

Nyoman had inspired the women. He had figured out on his own how to get funding for his water buffalo and his dream of lifting his family out of extreme poverty and dependence on the generosity of strangers. The women could see it was working and they wanted the same.

## Reaching Out With an Idea

It was not long after I returned home from this visit to the village that I received a fax from Freddy recounting his latest interaction with the women. Because of the uncertainty of communication lines, when the villagers wanted to meet with Freddy they would send a contact person to his place of work and ask him to visit the village. The women wanted to discuss their plan. This required a daylong journey for Freddy, but on his first day off he made the trip.

When Freddy arrived in the village, the women shared their plan to pay for the education of their children: they wanted to raise pigs. They wanted to duplicate a model they had seen or heard about in a neighboring village that had been supported by a U.S.-based nonprofit organization. The plan required the purchase of twenty piglets. They would build a fenced-in area to keep the piglets contained and safe, care for them, raise them, and at the right age, sell some to neighboring villages and harvest the others for their own village's consumption, enhancing the nutritional benefits for their families. In addition, they would use the pig manure to fertilize the rice fields and small gardens. They requested that Freddy relay this information to me, Ibu Marilyn, which he did in a fax as soon as he returned to Bali.

After studying the long, handwritten fax for several hours, I found their possibility thinking delightful and creative. Bursting with energy and excitement, I decided to phone Freddy to obtain more details; unfortunately, in my joyous state, I forgot that for him it would be the middle of the night. My phone call woke him and his whole family. He sleepily confirmed that I had read the information correctly, the village women were asking for funding to purchase twenty piglets. Freddy thought he could make the proper contacts to get the village women their piglets; the cost would be around $350, which included the fencing and food for about six months.

Freddy raised a question: Would this project eventually lead to the same advantages as the water buffalo?

It seemed a bit more complicated with many unpredictable variables. Would the women be able to raise enough money with their piglet venture to pay for the educations of their children? Neither of us knew with any certainty if this project would be successful or even what the women knew about raising pigs, but we were hopeful and did not want to dampen their entrepreneurial spirits.

With hope and enthusiasm, but also too many questions unanswered and unasked, we agreed to move forward. My thoughts immediately turned toward the towering question of funding and Freddy returned to his bed to complete his night's rest.

## Where to Get $350?

Once again, we were in the position of needing funds. Again, I was not comfortable going back to the traditional and loyal donors to fund such an enterprise. The donors were quite comfortable donating money for the education of children, and I did not want to do anything to jeopardize their confidence and trust.

From the donors' perspective, there is very limited risk to donating funds for education; the money goes directly to the school. It is the responsibility of the children and the parents to ensure their attendance, which could be verified annually through the school officials. Each year after my visit to Indonesia, I brought back pictures of the school children and the donors' confidence in the program grew. Because of this, I did not see these same donors as a viable source for community development funding. Perhaps my *other* source would come through again.

My family loves me. It also helped that my birthday was fast approaching. "Mom, what do you want for your birthday?" they asked.

Experiencing déjà vu, I blurted, "Twenty piglets. I mean, I need cash!"

"Okay, Mom," they answered, "what are you going to do with twenty piglets and why do you need cash?"

I longed for a less direct or better answer than "I want cash to buy twenty piglets," but nothing works like the truth. I produced yet another opportunity for my children to default to their sarcasm gene. After the litany of pig roasting and bacon jokes, I told them about our proverbial extended family of impoverished women in the Indonesian village and their plan to start a pig/pork enterprise. When my birthday arrived, so did a gift box containing three hundred and fifty $1 bills!

Soon, a fax was off to Freddy and the money was wired for the piglet project. Even though I was quite happy, it was hard for me to imagine the details and how long it might take to turn piglets into educational funds. A few weeks later, however, I was caught off guard when I received an email from Freddy with two photo attachments. It was unusual at that time to receive an email from Freddy because he did not have direct access to a computer, and the Internet was often down. The quality of the attached photos was grainy and it took a minute to realize what they were. In the first photograph, the women of the village were smiling and standing in a row, with the rainforest as a background, each holding a little piglet by its shoulder blades out in front of her. The second picture was of the piglets, along with the women and children holding a big sign that read "Happy Birthday Ibu Marilyn!" This was, by far, the best use of birthday cash ever! Those were the most adorable piglets I had ever seen, and by the end of the day I had given each of them a name. I could not stop smiling, and my family smiled with me.

### Luck and Good Fortune on Our Side, Again

Amazingly, the next spring when I visited the village the cute piglets had grown into large pigs and were not as adorable as their baby pictures. The pigs were fulfilling their intended purpose, which was to raise cash for the women of the village. Fewer mothers stood in line to have their children's names checked off our list. Instead there were many women who greeted me with a different attitude about them; they were proud. For the first time, I saw these women look into my eyes with self-assurance rather than the dependent hope that I would bring enough money for their children to attend school. The women were working hard, gathering food for the pigs, and constantly repairing the bamboo fencing. As the pigs grew and became stronger, they also became more curious, often pushing their way through the fencing. Caring for the pigs was not easy or clean work, but the women were up for the task—fueled by their desire for self-sufficiency.

The economy of the community was changing, and the villagers were leading the march into a future independent of charity. That year, 350 children were removed from my list of students; they no longer required outside donations for educational sponsorships to attend school!

## GO NEXT-DOOR TO BORROW

How many of us grew up with the chore to go next-door to borrow an egg, a cup of flour, a stick of butter ... whatever? Imagine if there were no eggs, flour, or butter in the neighborhood. That was the daily circumstance of the villagers: no neighbors with an extra egg, or for that matter any eggs, ever.

The same year I first saw the adult pigs—soon to be sold and/or harvested—the women of the village asked for a special meeting with Freddy and me. In their *possibility thinking* and newly found entrepreneurial spirit, they were considering purchasing hens and one rooster to launch another grassroots enterprise. Their plan was to purchase baby chicks to raise and then reap the benefits of having fresh eggs. The plan was to keep some of the eggs for their own use, serving to improve the nutritional health of their children, and sell the remaining eggs at the market, plus harvest some of the chickens to be sold to neighboring villages.

The goal of the women was to have the children learn to care for the chickens with adult supervision. The women would teach the children how to prepare salted eggs, which are sold on the streets as a snack or purchased to mix with a rice dish. Salted eggs are similar to the Western pickled eggs I remembered seeing in large jars in stores when I was a child. The

> For the first time, I saw these women look into my eyes with self-assurance rather than the dependent hope ...

salted egg process begins by carefully and slowly placing the eggs in a container about the size of a child's swimming pool that is filled with saltwater brine. Initially, the eggs float, but as they marinade and harden for thirty to forty days, the eggs sink to the bottom of the pool. When this occurs, the eggs are ready for eating. Seemed simple enough to me, although I am not a fan of salted eggs. The children agreed to care for the chickens, make and sell their salted eggs, and help contribute to the nutritional and economic growth of the family and the community. Their efforts also contributed to the funding of their education.

Less than $200 was needed to purchase the baby chicks, the food, and the fencing. As you might guess, the funding came from my ever-patient and generous family. The chickens were purchased from a neighboring village in the region and yet another grassroots enterprise was launched.

## A BRAVE NEW VILLAGE

In the next three years, the residents of the village became totally self-sustaining in raising the funds for the education of their children. The mothers were no longer waiting to see if someone from another country would appear with enough money to send their children to school. And, along with economic self-sufficiency, they gained self-respect through having a voice in creating their own solutions. Their solutions brought dignity, confidence, pride in accomplishment, and hope in controlling their own destiny. They had lost their sense of dependency on outsiders—and that seemed like a wonderful trade-off to me.

> These villagers were teaching me a different formula for success that entailed me gathering resources to provide them the opportunity to help themselves.

It was gratifying to see Nyoman continually working in the rice field with the water buffalo, Ibu Marilyn, and the community pride taken in the pork enterprise as well as the chickens. The village was changing and so, too, my thinking and my heart. My thoughts about how to really help people through the use of humanitarian aid were evolving as dramatically as the village.

Before these experiences, the formula to success in aid projects was pretty straightforward: identify the need, gather the resources (usually money), and fill the need. Whenever I could get others interested in projects and successfully gather money from donors, I felt empowered and it was gratifying to think of myself as helping and creating positive change in the world. I often told myself that anything I do is better than doing nothing. While that may be true, I was learning there might be more beneficial methods of doing.

These villagers were teaching me a different formula for success that entailed me gathering resources to provide them the opportunity to help themselves. They were proving that they were capable of finding their own solutions to poverty. And the process empowered *them*—rather than me. I witnessed the shift of empowerment from donors to people who no longer waited with the hope that others would help. Rather, they were people who arrived at their own solutions, leading the way with excitement and determination, walking with respect and dignity. This new path we were walking together was much more satisfying and rewarding to all of us.

My journey toward understanding and promoting sustainable giving had begun. "Does she really want to help?" had been answered, but there was so much more for me to learn about sustainability. The next lessons on this journey would come when my volunteer efforts took me to Romania.

## LESSONS LEARNED

1. **Their pride shines brightest.**

   The pride of providing education for their children looked much better on the faces of parents in the village than it ever did on mine, Freddy's, or even the donors.

2. **Lend a hand, not a handout.**

   Given the opportunity, the villagers were able to identify their own solutions to poverty. They were eager to work hard and earn the necessary money to pay for the education of their children.

3. **There are always unintentional consequences of giving.**

   The unintentional consequence of our expression of goodwill through donated funds was actually causing harm by creating a dependency of the villagers on donors. Ultimately this robbed the villagers of the opportunity to gain self-esteem, dignity, and self-respect; this was not helpful. Dependency on well-intended, generous donors does not equate to sustainability of a program.

4. **Don't be naïve.**

Freddy and I were extremely naïve in our purchase of the livestock for the villagers. Just handing animals over to them, assuming they would know how to care for the animals and become successful entrepreneurs may have been well intentioned, but banking on luck did not become a solid plan for future programs.

5. **Beginner's luck is just that—luck; don't count on it.**

I do not recommend anyone duplicate our approach as described in this chapter. This is not an example of how to accomplish a successful sustainable program. We were blessed with beginner's luck as we got caught up in the energy of the moment. We were fortunate to not be blindsided by any number of things that could have gone wrong. Nyoman might not have taken proper care of his water buffalo, resulting in losing it. The villagers might have immediately harvested the piglets as part of a big village pig roast. (I have heard of such happenings.) They might not have grown into healthy adult pigs that would reproduce and be sold for profit. The same could have happened to the chickens.

There are professional humanitarian organizations that know exactly how to implement community development through livestock and/or agricultural projects. There are organizations that understand what the environment will support and they work with the recipients, teaching them how to care for the animals to ensure good health, proper living conditions, appropriate harvesting methods, and that the intended impact of sustainability is achieved.

6. **Clear goals and objectives are needed.**
   We learned that before beginning a project we needed to have clear goals and objectives. This project began with the expectation of funding the education of twenty children for one year. With uncontrolled project creep, the number quickly grew to 250 children, then 500 children, and finally to 1,200 children. We had no exit strategy and just kept digging deeper, requiring more and more funding. It was the impoverished villagers who developed a plan that would help themselves and ultimately help us get out of our self-made quicksand of a project.

7. **Give, but with conditions.**
   Every resource we provided to this village was a charitable gift. It was not necessary to *give* them the water buffalo, the piglets, or the chickens; we could have negotiated a microloan to fund the purchase of the animals by the villagers. The advantage of lending them the money rather than simply giving it is that the proceeds of the loan repayment could then be used as a revolving fund to assist neighbors or neighboring villages with further economic development based on a sustainable lending model.

8. **Ask first.**
   Freddy and I saw a problem. We read *The Annual United Nations Report: The Status of the World's Children (2000)*, and made the decision to identify a rural, impoverished village in Indonesia in order to provide educational

funds for some of the children. Looking back, I wonder, What if we had asked the residents of the village if they wanted their children to receive an education? What were they willing to do to ensure that their children receive an education? Would they have implemented a community development plan? What resources would they have needed to implement their plan?

*"Always bear in mind that your own resolution to success is more important than any other."*

CHAPTER THREE

# THE COMPASS SWINGS, THE LESSONS CONTINUE

I was invited to spend seven weeks in Romania to work with a service organization. The intent of the visit was to assist the organization in identifying community needs and then collectively work our way through the grant-writing maze in an attempt to fund desperately needed projects. To maneuver successfully through the grant-submission process, one must fully understand what is and is not grantable, according to the general foundation guidelines as well as the philosophy and intended impact of the foundation offering the potential grant. For this effort, the grant source was an international foundation based in the United States, and we followed their guidelines.

Though I had plenty of experience identifying projects and writing grants, this excursion presented a significant and very different learning curve—one that I was not fully prepared for. The curve was not about the nuances of grant writing but rather about discovery and opening the minds of those in need to reach further than they had ever been able to reach before.

## GETTING THERE

I planned the trip to Romania, stubbornly dismissing suggestions from others who were familiar with the area. These seasoned travelers were more than willing to help me with arrangements, but I decided it was best to find my own way. I planned to arrive a few days early in order to explore the historic city that was to become my temporary home. Once the clock began ticking on the intense, seven-week period of consultation, there would be no time for sightseeing. In preparation for the work, I corresponded with the host service organization, requesting that they begin the process of identifying potential projects and needs and associated solutions.

Most of my travel arrangements were fairly routine and without complications, but the final leg of my journey required a driver—a little more difficult than booking the air travel, but after multiple email exchanges with a travel agent in Romania, I was pretty sure I had found a driver.

After landing in Romania, I waited for the driver to pick me up. I was just beginning to wonder if perhaps I should have accepted some help with arrangements when a young man holding a cardboard sign with my name on it appeared. This was a very young driver indeed—he looked all of fourteen. However, his presence seemed to confirm that I had successfully soloed through the requisition of my overland transportation requirement. While the driver was punctual, I quickly learned that in addition to his youthfulness, he did not speak English. Since I do not speak Romanian, our initial exchange was little more than gestures, smiles, and feeble attempts to convey what was not conveyable.

The transportation that I had so confidently arranged turned out to be a very small, old car with character. Because of its size, my luggage barely fit, and as I sat with one suitcase on my lap and two more crowded next to me on the seat, I realized once again I had over packed (a life lesson that has yet to fully sink in). Off we went.

It was January, with lots of snow and bone-chilling temperatures, so it was an interesting ride with no heat and a hole in the floorboard that provided a nice view of the road passing underneath us. When we hit a bump, which was quite often, icy slush splattered up through the hole. Add to that road rage, which it turns out is universal. Throughout the trip, the young driver remained silent ... except when we encountered a slow-moving cart or an animal or any other vehicle impeding our progress. His rage was like the tide, starting with a rant that then climaxed as we overtook the obstacle or impediment, then gradually subsided into mumbled, barely audible words that gave way once again to silence.

As we drove out of Bucharest into the rural, agricultural areas, it seemed as if life and energy were slowing down. We passed many travelers in their donkey- or horse-drawn wagons, often carrying what appeared to be large families and all their possessions. More people walked alongside of the wagons. They walked the road from one village to another, wearing what appeared to be untreated and untailored animal skins with hanging fur. Initially, the procession of people and carts reminded me of the wagon trains in old Western movies. In those movies people were often heading toward a better tomorrow, which unfortunately may not have been the destination of the travelers I observed. In addition to the wagons and people, we also shared the road with herds of animals kept mostly intact by their accompanying shepherds. With no designated road crossings, we were frequently forced into long waits as the herds made their way from one side of the road to the other—at their own pace. No special attention was given to motorized vehicles; rather there was a continual and often fragile intermixing of all that traveled the road.

After a much lengthier trip than I had anticipated, we finally made our way into the destination city: old, beautiful, and bearing the marks of bygone centuries. The driver maneuvered through the narrow streets and then stopped abruptly. As my luggage and I tumbled out of the vehicle, I had my first look at my temporary residence. What had no doubt once been a grand, ornate building, taller than the adjacent structures, now appeared very old, very tired, and lacking the maintenance and attention it deserved.

My room was on the fourth floor of the building, while most of our grant-related business meetings and conferences would take place on the first floor. It seemed as if I was always forgetting something in my room, so daily trips up and down the stairs became the norm. The building was only open during office hours, with a steady stream of visitors, but in the evening the structure became quiet and rather lonely. Most of my evenings were devoted to completing paperwork and planning as many activities as possible for the next day. The people and organization representatives I needed to meet with often came to the building. This saved me from arranging transportation or, if I attempted a foot trip, the inevitable realization that I was lost. (Without a doubt, I am "directionally challenged.")

Being from Northern Michigan and accustomed to cold weather, I'd assumed adverse weather conditions would not be an issue for me. However, I was soon to learn that the constant rain and snow, as well as the damp Romanian cold, chilled me to the bone. Each night, I would climb into bed wearing my heavy flannel pajamas only to discover the next morning that during the night I had managed to add several layers of pants, jeans, sweaters, and/or sweatshirts. The daylight hours were short. Even during the day, the village was surrounded by shades of gray; it was like living in an old black-and-white movie.

## SORTING THROUGH THE NEEDS

At the time of my visit, Romania was in its tenth year of a new, evolving democratic government that came about after the overthrow of Communist rule. The citizens were eager to explore, learn, and practice their new freedoms, whether in the hope of economic growth or to build social service programs for their citizens in need. Many social-aid agencies had emerged in an effort to do the service work the Communist government had once provided to some but not all. Under the Communist government, neighbor was suspicious of neighbor, wondering if the other was providing information to the government in return for greater rewards. This suspicion was now conditioned into the people, shackling them and was slow to be cast off. Another lingering effect of the Communist government was a general reluctance or hesitation to fully reach out in an effort to achieve that which had not been a remote possibility before. The government had stymied people's ability to dream and hope for what might be within their reach.

Soon after arriving and prior to any tour of the village, a team of service organization members, local community leaders, and I met to discuss the process for final identification of potential humanitarian-aid projects that might be grantable. At our first meeting, I asked the spokesperson for the local service organization to show me their list of community needs and potential solutions. Since they had been working on the list for a few weeks, I assumed it would be lengthy and detailed, so I was both surprised and a little confused at its contents. The list was short, reflected items that would not meet the criteria for the grant money we were seeking, and listed no sustainable projects. Instead, items included a building, salaries, and a few generic items of medical equipment.

As I came to know and better understand those I worked with in the village, and we were able to visit the various projects, the lists of requirements evolved into more specific items, in line with the available grant money. Constrained thinking, conditioned through decades of idea suppression by the Communist government, gave way to the art of reaching for the possible. The list of projects and needs could have been endless, as this village and its nation faced monumental challenges. Every visit to a potential project was an emotional event: encouraging, disheartening, sometimes inspiring, and occasionally overwhelming. We visited orphanages, homes for unwed mothers, elderly centers, and schools.

Public schools receive little government funding. As a result, the textbooks were long outdated and many of the once beautiful school buildings appeared rundown and ill-equipped. Multiple students shared a single desk, often crowding three students into a desk meant for two. School supplies were almost nonexistent. Teachers received approximately $50 per month; so it was necessary that they give private teaching sessions in the evenings to supplement their incomes and support their families. Many parents voiced their suspicions that teachers were not teaching enough during the normal school hours in order to ensure that the students required additional tutoring in the evening—at the parents' expense.

The health-care system seemed to match that of education. Hospitals lacked an adequate number of patient rooms, along with appropriate medical equipment and medicines. Medical supplies always fell short of the constant need. The average salary for a hospital doctor was $100 per month, so when given opportunities elsewhere, many doctors chose to leave. Every day there were long lines of parents and children waiting for the too few doctors to see them at the limited health-care facilities.

Pregnant women were not allowed hospital admission until they reached a certain stage of labor. Sometimes women walked as far as twenty miles from their villages in order to give birth there. With no money for transportation, they began the long walk early, arriving a week or so ahead of the obligatory labor time. They would then sleep on the street just outside of the hospital until they could be admitted. When they did give birth, they were only allowed to stay in the hospital a few hours, after which they returned to the streets to begin the long walk back to their village—this time with a newborn. Some women and their families were so poor that they could not purchase a protective blanket to wrap around their babies.

During our project discovery process associated with these impoverished, pregnant women, we learned of some small, very special, nonprofit organizations doing wonderful and important work. A group of local women had begun putting together diaper-bag kits for the new mothers to ensure that they would have the basic essentials required for a new baby. The kits included a wrapping blanket, diapers, nutritional supplements, and soaps. There was another organization that opened a home with just a few rooms. The rooms were occupied briefly by either pregnant women waiting for their time to be admitted to the hospital or new mothers regaining their strength before returning to their villages. While in the home, the women received an introduction to infant care and other related health issues, but only a very limited amount of information could be transferred to them because their stays were so brief.

One of the special places we visited was a home for unwed mothers and orphans. At the time, Eastern Europe had more than 200,000 orphans living in institutions, and all foreign adoptions had been stopped. The cessation was an effort to end the black-market industry of selling babies under the guise of adoption. This corrupt practice encouraged teen pregnancy and often resulted in harm to the young, unwed mothers. Most of the impoverished mothers in the home for unwed mothers and orphans were poor, homeless girls. Some had been residents of this orphanage for an extended period of time; some had been abused and raped on the streets and were now seeking refuge. If the mothers chose not to give their babies up for adoption, they were able to keep their infants with them in the orphanage as they tried to learn survival and infant-care skills. New mothers and teenage girls who had been raised in the orphanage and chose to leave were often doing so with no money, no life or job skills, and no understanding of what is required to exist in the world. They were totally vulnerable on the streets.

> We sought the final why or the root cause of it all ...

As we visited the various places and projects in need, we tried our best to gain an understanding of the circumstances that had led to what we witnessed. We sought the final why or the root cause of it all, because this information could be used to add value and strength to the grant application. I so appreciated and respected these individuals and nonprofit organizations. They were trying to help with so few assets. Their efforts were to be applauded, and each and every potential project could benefit from grant money that might be sought on their behalf.

Deciding which projects would be selected for grant submission and which ones would not became one of the hardest decisions we faced. Some of the projects were eliminated because they did not meet the criteria set by the granting institution. When faced with that situation, it is always difficult to explain to those seeking assistance that their project could not be funded. The look on their faces showed hope dashed, disappointment, and sometimes frustration with those who supposedly came to help. For those projects that did meet the guidelines, a grant-writing effort of marathon proportions took place, which was only possible with the help of the members of the service organization as well as incredible support by the nonprofit organizations themselves. Collectively, we were able to complete and forward a significant number of grant requests.

Then, began the wait.


## SUCCESS BUT NOT SUSTAINABILITY

We were ecstatic to learn that every single one of our grant requests was approved. Congratulations and praise was freely expressed, but I knew there was no time to rest on our laurels. While all of the grants—which collectively provided medical equipment, school supplies, and nourishment for infants—brought temporary relief and support, none promoted sustainability. Medical equipment must be maintained and there was no budget for inspections, maintenance, or replacement of components. School supplies funded would meet the needs of the school for a *single* year, which was also the length of time for the infant-nourishment program. Without sustainability, the cycle of annual or seasonal fundraising and grant writing was destined to continue, always with the possibility of insufficient funds and subsequent drastic cuts to much-needed programs.

The concept of and need for sustainable programs had been discussed at length with those I had worked with so closely. Even short-term projects, such as purchasing equipment, would require upkeep, indicating the need for a long-term funding strategy. With each round of discussions, sometimes extending well into the evening after a long day, I sought to challenge their thinking both in terms of going beyond their immediate, short-term requirements and the need for or value of sustainable projects, but I was never sure if the message was understood ... until I met Sophia.

## *A Sustainable Project, Or So We Thought*

Sophia was a young, energetic social worker who was especially interested in the concept of sustainable humanitarian-aid projects. We met often, usually at a small corner café where we would consume the favorite local soup and fresh bread, to discuss at length the importance of sustainable projects. Sophia's generation was experiencing both frustration and opportunity. Many were choosing to leave Romania, impatient with the slow process of making much-needed changes and in search of better opportunities. Others, like Sophia, wanted to stay and help lead the change in their country. These young, educated, motivated citizens represented the future—and they were inspiring.

Soon after I returned home, Sophia phoned with excitement and great energy. She was in the process of developing an educational program for teenage girls who needed funding to attend school. Sophia was quite pleased with herself, having kept sustainability in mind as she designed the project: a small bread bakery that would be run by the girls in the program. Sophia explained that the girls would learn to bake, market, and sell the bread, eventually earning enough money to pay for their own educational expenses. I became as excited as Sophia, offering her encouragement and reinforcement. This appeared to be a perfect example of a sustainable project, but we were to learn along the way, enthusiasm clouded our vision.

In order to launch the project, an oven was needed, but not just any oven. The oven had to be constructed with a special type of stone so it could be used outside. The cost to build it was approximately $500. Because of time constraints, it was not realistic to go through the drawn-out process of grant writing and waiting. So, in the zeal of my enthusiasm and with a strong desire for Sophia to keep moving, I decided to personally fund this oven project. It was only $500; she would have the funds by the next morning. Sophia was grateful and proud that her thinking and actions were on a sustainable track. I was proud of Sophia. I felt as if my mentorship and quest to promote sustainable projects were coming to fruition. Within a couple weeks, Sophia faxed pictures of the stone oven surrounded by smiling young girls.

However, my euphoria over Sophia's ability to design and implement a sustainable project was interrupted in less than a month. Early one morning, in a soft, sad voice, she informed me that the oven had been vandalized. Her agency agreed to pay for the repairs but only if a fence was built around the oven area to protect it from further damage. The estimated cost for building the fence was $600—more than the cost of the oven. The need was urgent and once again I agreed to fund the fence. It seemed necessary and appropriate in order to protect the initial investment.

Unfortunately, this was not the last of Sophia's SOS calls. Those that followed included requirements for additional funding to purchase baking utensils and ingredients, then more money to hire someone to teach the girls how to make bread and market it. By the time the bread hit the street, the initial startup funding was nearly $3,000 and the return on our investment would take even longer than anticipated.

Ironically or perhaps regrettably, the finger of fault for this less-than-fully-thought-out sustainable effort was squarely pointed at me—the woman promoting the value of sustainable projects; the woman with an MBA who knew how to work the numbers and was certainly capable of helping Sophia develop a business plan. There were only a few key critical questions that I should have asked to prevent this financial sprawl. But, I was too caught up in the excitement of the moment and naïvely thought the $500 would be the beginning and end of the startup money. It was an expensive and important lesson that Sophia learned. But learning my own lessons required some repetition.

### With the Best of Intentions

From the beginning of my stay in the village, I would leave my apartment to venture out in the evening, sometimes just to clear my head, take in some fresh air, or join colleagues for dinner. There were several Peace Corps workers staying in the same town and it was entertaining and interesting to talk with them about their personal journey to help others. Often on my strolls, I was approached by what appeared to be poor street children begging for money. It was almost impossible to say no, but if I gave money to one child, I soon was surrounded by a large group of children, who were followed by an elderly group—everyone begging for money. The children looked pale, as if they were all suffering from the same illness, and hungry. Some wore a sweater or a jacket, which never appeared adequate to protect them from the cold, and some wore no outer layer of protective clothing. Instead, they wore multiple shirts and stood with one hand stuffed in a pant pocket and the other reaching out for money. All of the children had dark circles under their eyes as though they were sleep deprived. The repeated scenes of begging children became increasingly difficult and made going out in the evening for a meeting or dinner just about impossible; it was unthinkable to walk past them without giving them something. Before leaving the apartment I would plant single dollars or coins in my pockets, and I became so accustomed to doling out money that I could walk with a colleague, keep pace, and not interrupt the conversation as I fed the hands of children, the elderly, and teenagers. Whether I stayed home in my cold apartment or ventured out with an associate, every evening I worried about the hungry children. My nights became restless as I thought about their circumstances while I lay in my semi-comfortable bed.

It did not take long for me to come up with what I believed was a worthwhile, foolproof plan of action that would fulfill my need to help hungry children and their need to have food. I would collect/purchase day-old bread from the local bakeries and give it to the children when they approached me for money. I believed this would also benefit the store owners by keeping the children from coming into their shops and begging. If it was a successful program, a local organization would surely adopt the model, and we could write a grant to continue funding it after my departure.

The first voice of resistance to this foolproof plan was

my ever-present translator. He had proved to be a very good resource, teaching me about the culture and guiding me to ensure that I was respectful of local conditions; so I was surprised when he did not immediately and overwhelmingly endorse my plan. But instead of fully investigating why he was resistive, I willfully forged ahead.

My translator and I visited the bakeries, and he reluctantly helped me speak with the owners, asking them to sell me their leftover bread at a discounted price or, better, donate the aging baked goods to this new project in order to provide food to hungry children on the street. I had witnessed many storeowners tell the poor, begging children to leave their shops and to stop harassing customers.

For several evenings in a row my disgruntled translator and I stood in the rain and snow on a town square corner handing day-old bakery products to the hungry children. This felt so much better than trying to ignore the children's pleas or witnessing the translator shoo the children away. I was never sure what the translator said to the children as we handed them food, but he did not sound warm, friendly, or inviting. After just two consecutive nights, the children became accustomed to me being on the town square. By the third night, the crowd of begging children and elderly had doubled and was becoming more aggressive in their requests for assistance. Upon receiving anything—money or bread—the children would take it, immediately run away, but return a short time later. I never saw them actually eat the bread, and there was no real interaction between the children and me.

On our fourth night on the town square, my translator began to somewhat reluctantly share what was going on. When the children grabbed the bread or money and ran out of sight, usually just around the corner of the building, they met an older child or a parent who was waiting behind the building, and whatever the child collected from me was immediately given to that individual. In fact, the child who received the bread or money rarely shared in its rewards. The translator said that some of these children would be physically beaten if they did not collect a specific amount of money every day; the bread was no substitute for cash.

With each passing evening, the children were becoming more insistent on receiving money rather than bread. In an effort to counter their insistence and to ensure the children would receive some of the nutrition they needed, I came up with an addendum to my plan. Through the translator, I told the children that in order to be given the bread, they must consume it while standing in front of us. This seemed to be the only way I could be sure the bread was going into their bellies and not someone else's. It was disheartening that under these new terms, most of the children refused the bread, begged for money, and when they did not receive it slowly walked away.

> I should have given greater credence to what my translator was telling me from the beginning.

Within a fortnight, my grand plan for feeding the children was in shambles. I hadn't truly listened to those whose home or village I was visiting. I should have given greater credence to what my translator was telling me from the beginning; I should have fully realized the impact of my actions on him. He would be living in this village long after my departure. Looking back, I imagine that I must have appeared rather righteous and arrogant to him, acting as though local people did not understand there were hungry children on the street. Though I will never know for sure, perhaps in his translating efforts with the bakers, he was apologizing for my insensitive behavior as well as conveying my request to the storeowners.

It was a heartbreaking reality check and a bit humbling for me to realize how very complicated solutions to hunger and poverty can be, and that I did not have all the answers. With this sincere but misguided effort, I had learned yet another lesson about the complexity of humanitarian aid.

### Postscript: Caring Hearts

My visit to this Eastern European country began in late January following the horrific terrorist attacks of 9/11 in the United States. Throughout my stay, as I visited the homeless, the poor, and those in need, the people would consistently pause the conversation and change the focus to extend to me their heartfelt sympathy regarding the tragedy suffered in my home country. They would often embrace me as their eyes filled with tears. Through an interpreter or in slow, hesitant, broken English, they all asked about the well-being of my fellow citizens in America. A local artist created a beautiful oil painting of the two towers at the World Trade Center with a rising sun in the background that he presented to me as a gift. He wanted everyone who saw the painting to remember the beauty of the towers and feel assured that one day the deep wounds of 9/11 would be healed.

> How humbling it was to experience the sincerity of the people, so concerned about the welfare of the United States and its citizens.

How humbling it was to experience the sincerity of the people, so concerned about the welfare of the United States and its citizens. They momentarily set aside their difficulties to offer their hearts in comfort to a hurting America. We each shed tears and held onto hope for the other.

## Lessons Learned

1. **Learn the rules.**

   To maneuver successfully through the grant writing and submission process, one must fully understand what is and is not grantable according to the general foundation guidelines as well as the philosophy and intended impact of the foundation offering the potential grant.

2. **Communicate with a common understanding.**

   This is a valuable lesson that I have found myself learning over and over. When I requested that the local service organization begin the process of identifying potential projects, we did not share a common understanding of what might be possible. I assumed that their thinking would be the same as mine, but we did not reach a meeting of the minds until after several discussions.

3. **Use every opportunity.**

   Rather than just provide temporary shelter for the pregnant women or those preparing to return to their villages after delivery, the nonprofit organization running the home for women used this brief opportunity to impart basic educational knowledge to new mothers. The women received an introduction to infant care and other related health issues.

4. **Seek out the root cause.**

   It is vital to fully explore and understand the root cause of a problem or situation. As we visited the various projects, *why* questions were asked until we felt we had reached the core or root cause of the problem. Professionals in the field of quality believe that asking "why" five times will get you there.

## 5. Think projects through.

Before funding the bakery oven, I should have thought the project through in greater detail. Had I asked Sophia a few key questions, we would have had a much more complete assessment of the project and known all the fiscal requirements to get it up and running on its way to sustainability.

*"The object of education is to prepare the young to educate themselves throughout their lives."*

ROBERT M. HUTCHINS

CHAPTER FOUR

# A NEGOTIATED AGREEMENT

In 2004, a friend and I cofounded a small foundation. From the outset, the foundation's goal was to provide aid to needy organizations in developing countries by helping them capitalize on their sustainable humanitarian-aid projects. In an effort to determine which project we would first aid, I began a preliminary search online, and ultimately traveled to Guatemala. We were aware of a large, longstanding, aid organization in Guatemala that was involved in the type of projects that interested us, and our first step was to visit one of these projects. After observing what was going on, it became apparent that the amount of money our foundation had available to contribute would not make a significant impact to aid the programs run by this organization. The dedicated people there recommended a new and worthy project focused on providing education to the children who lived with their families at the municipal dump.

This new, much smaller project was ultimately the first one selected by our foundation to support. After numerous personal visits and continual communication with the program director, I came to know the program well, but from a different perspective than that given me by my firsthand involvement with so many other projects. This experience offered me an opportunity to step back and begin to see both the successes and shortcomings of other projects. The story that unfolds below is told both from the perspective of what I experienced and the experiences shared with me by the program director. Each of us benefited from the experience and knowledge of the other, and together we were able to learn important lessons about sustainable programs. This program director was my first teacher in negotiating with the economically poor.

At our initial meeting, the program director and I took the first of many trips to the Guatemala City dump; every time it was a gut-wrenching experience. The reality is that many of the people we met there—whose faces filled my dreams—are destined to spend their entire lives at this dumpsite.

There are hundreds of city dumps scattered throughout Central America; the one in Guatemala City is the largest—the size of approximately ten football fields. Living and working conditions at the dumpsites are horrendous by any country's standards. The air is fetid with toxic smoke from the endless small fires of burning garbage, plastics, and rubber. It is dangerous for any living being to breathe this air. Predators, large and small, human and non-human, often cause harm to each other, as various species patrol the dump in search of food. Toddlers get into a tug-of-war with stray dogs for a scrap of food; both are hungry. Huge vultures swoop down among the rats, stray dogs search through animal and human waste and dead animal carcasses, all desperately sharing a common goal to end their hunger. There is always a pungent, unforgettable stench in the air that leaves an unaccustomed visitor like me gasping. What others have discarded is often the single source of daily food and opportunity for income to approximately 10,000 people who gather at the dump every day. The search for food is never-ending, as is the collecting of items such as wire, glass, and paper that are sold to the recyclers for a few pennies. Sustenance requires the efforts of all family members—even the youngest and smallest. Of the 10,000 residents who live at the edge of the dump, 6,000 are children.

Most of the children are partially clothed and exhibit obvious signs of malnutrition with thinning hair and/or large bald spots on their heads. Some of their hair has turned an auburn color from lack of nutrition; many have open sores. They

> This experience offered me an opportunity to step back and begin to see both the successes and shortcomings of other projects.

have bloated, swollen bellies. The children have never had a bath or experienced clean water running over their hands or even tasted uncontaminated water. Many of the children are lethargic. Most of the children living at or near the dump have never consumed a healthy meal, only having access to food that has been discarded as trash by others.

## EDUCATING THE CHILDREN

### Breaking Through the Obstacles

Under these prevailing conditions, families living at the Guatemala City dump do not seriously consider the possibility of their children attending school; it would be little more than a passing dream that could never come true, for two very significant reasons. While the government supports public schools in Guatemala, and the tuition is free, the families must pay for school uniforms, books, and supplies, all at a cost of approximately $100 per year. This is an unachievable astronomical goal and an economic impossibility for the families living at the dump, especially considering that most families have more than one child. Secondly, if the children were in school each day, they would not be available to help sift through the garbage in search of food and recyclable materials for the family to sell to vendors. Removing the children from this endless daily routine would mean the suffering of the entire family.

Any attempt to provide tuition assistance and place the children in school had to address the negative impact of removing one participant from the family's search for resources. Even if the obstacles of tuition and food could be overcome, there was another barrier to conquer: the local school administrators were opposed to the idea. When they were first approached, they were resistant to any possibility of placing these particular children in their school. Since the children living in the area of the dump had never attended school, there was a requirement that each child be evaluated to ensure placement at the proper grade level. This task would require considerable time from the school personnel— time they felt they did not have. The administrators knew that some of the new teenage students would be evaluated at the pre-literate level with five- and six-year-old children. Their life experiences were not even typical of poor Guatemalan children. But, after lengthy discussions and persuasive arguments, the administrators agreed to evaluate and ultimately permit a limited number of children from this impoverished area to attend their school, if they had the proper uniforms, books, and school supplies.

## Education for Groceries

The program director conducted many informal surveys while walking around the dump, casually becoming familiar with the families and asking the children if they wanted to attend school. Although her question always elicited an affirmative answer from the children, who were desperate and eager for an education, they had about them a foreboding sense of hopelessness. They were rarely exposed to people outside of their environment, and neither their parents nor grandparents had attended school, so they seemed to accept as their destiny conditions of abject poverty and illiteracy. Witnessing such young children with no sparkle in their tired eyes, no dreams of what to be when I grow up weighed heavily on this young program director.

Nevertheless, there was a plan for tuition and surplus food solidly in the works, as well as the unenthusiastic acceptance of the school administrators, so many of the obstacles to educating the children had been overcome ... or so the inexperienced Western program director thought. The plan was straightforward. The initial tuition money came from the pockets of the program director and her circle of friends and family back home. She believed that she would be able to obtain future funding from people when they heard the story of these eager but poor children. If the families living at the dump agreed to send their child to school—with perfect attendance for one week—they would receive a bag of groceries. The program director was able to garner the support of many local volunteers from church groups to coordinate with small, family-owned food stores to donate one bag of groceries weekly for the family of each child enrolled in the program. The bag of groceries was intended to fill the food-gathering void caused by the child's absence while attending school. The importance of each child attending school daily was emphatically stressed, and a volunteer social worker accepted the task of tracking attendance and liaising between the program manager and the school.

The local Guatemalan volunteers had successfully negotiated the terms for becoming a member of the education program; they came to agreements with the school administrators, the storeowners, and now the families and the children themselves. Several dozen families and children were interviewed and twelve children were finally chosen by the program director and local volunteers to become the inaugural class of the informally named "groceries for education" program. With so many of the pieces in place, some of the families and the children now had the opportunity to dare to dream.

Prior to their first day of school, the children were given their new uniforms, books, and a backpack containing school supplies. This was the first time they had owned a pencil, paper, shoes, or a new article that had not come from the local city dump. The program director said the children seemed happy, excited, and even joyful, but also a little confused, scared, and intimidated by the prospect of participating in a structured school with teachers and other children. Many of these families had never left the city dump area because of the collective rejection, open ridicule, and prejudice of the general population. The anxiety of the children was understandable, but it did not overpower their strong desire to step forward.

At the end of the first week, the program appeared to be working well with only a few mishaps. The children were totally unaccustomed to sitting still in a classroom at a desk for a few hours at a time, but all twelve had perfect attendance and were the recipients of support and mentorship from the local volunteers and appointed school liaison. On Friday at the end of the school week, the twelve mothers representing the families involved in the program came to the humble program office—recycled card tables and broken chairs in a boarded-up building at the edge of the city dump—where they collected their bags of groceries.

Unfortunately, the next few weeks did not go as well; in fact, they did not go at all. Each week became an increasing test of wills and commitment to the terms of the agreement. Early in the second week, the school liaison knew that there was not perfect attendance by all twelve children. The program director and the volunteers supporting the program were concerned and did not know what to do. The negotiated agreement was "one week of perfect school attendance for one bag of groceries on Friday." Although most of the children had only sporadically attended, the last school day of the second week, all twelve mothers stood in a group outside of the program's office to receive their groceries. Had they misunderstood or misinterpreted the agreement? "No," said the local volunteers, "the families understood the terms." Going against all that she felt, the program director found the courage to tell these families that they would not receive a bag of groceries; a bag of groceries would be given only to families that had children in school every day of the week. With blank faces, the mothers exchanged only a few words with one another. The children—neither dressed in their new uniforms nor carrying the backpacks—looked confused and slowly walked away with their mothers. This scene, as recounted by the program director, was heartbreaking and her courage to stand by the negotiated agreement exceeded even her expectations.

The third week was a repeat of week two. Only about half of the children were in school Monday and Tuesday; none had perfect attendance by the end of the week. The volunteer school liaison checked with the school's administrators daily. It seemed as though the groceries for education program was sinking rapidly and destined for failure. The morale of the volunteers was plummeting and the program director was beginning to question the integrity of the program. In addition, the school administrators were frustrated. They had completed all the evaluation work to place children in the proper classes, and now they were not attending. The owners of the contributing grocery stores wondered why the groceries they had set aside were not being collected as agreed.

Friday afternoon of the third week, the mothers and children gathered a short distance from the office. The program director and volunteers were surprised; after last week's rejection of their request for groceries and the agreement being again defined, how could they show up for groceries? In a rather bold and unpredicted act, the children changed their clothing, donned the school uniform, and proceeded to the program office with the mothers remaining at a distance in the background. Each child requested their family's bag of groceries, acting as if they were just returning from school. Standing her ground, and with the support of several volunteers, the director told the children no, and again explained the terms of the agreement: the only way to receive a bag of groceries next Friday was to have a week of perfect attendance in school for the coming week.

The children did not turn and quietly walk away as their mothers had the week before; they remained in front of the director and asked several more times for the food. The program director had never imagined how painful it would be to turn away hungry children in order to maintain the principles of a negotiated agreement. She was tempted to hand over the groceries, and it was only the local volunteers who stood between the heart of the program director, the groceries, and the children; this was requiring far more self-discipline than she thought she was capable of displaying.

After one successful week and two almost impossible weeks, the fourth week of the program brought renewed optimism. From the very first day, children walked past the program's office, wearing their school uniforms, on their way to attend school. As the week progressed, it was clear that some of the families were abiding by the agreement and would receive their groceries on Friday. By the end of the week, eight of the twelve children had attended school every day, yet all twelve mothers and children arrived to receive the groceries. While it was

> The program director had never imagined how painful it would be to turn away hungry children in order to maintain the principles of a negotiated agreement.

joyful and positive to present the eight families with their bag of groceries, it was extremely difficult and painful to see the other four families walk away empty-handed.

Week five was a testimony to the will of the program director to stand her ground. When Friday arrived, all twelve children had perfect attendance and received their groceries.

Because of these twelve children and the resoluteness of the first program director, the program continues today, supporting the educational needs of 345 children. This took years of incredibly hard work, the willingness of donors, continual refinement of the groceries for education program process, and the boundless dedication of the directors and volunteers.

## Lessons Learned

1. **Respect.**

   When the beneficiaries are given respect and acknowledged as major stakeholders in a program, involved in the process of integrative negotiation, they are invested in the success of the project.

2. **Consistency matters.**

   The consistency of the program director, with the moral support of the local volunteers, proved to be the single greatest factor contributing to the success of the program. Had the terms of the negotiated agreement between the families and the program been compromised, success would not have been achieved.

3. **Local knowledge is imperative.**

   Local knowledge supersedes and/or trumps any university degree. Whatever the outside experts assume they know about the needs of the people in the area truly pales when compared to depth of local knowledge.

# PART II

## FROM THE FIELD TO THE CLASSROOM AND BACK AGAIN

*"Nobody can go back and start a new beginning,*
*but anyone can start today and make a new ending."*
MARIA ROBINSON

# Introduction

When traveling life's journeys–whether personal, professional, or following our passions–the pathway taken may include an unexpected detour. If we are fortunate, reaching the end of the detour will also bring with it greater clarity to that which we seek, a sharper focus on the destination and a smoother, straighter path to continue onward. My unexpected and fortunate detour was one that took me from the villages back to the classroom and is chronicled in the following four chapters.

Chapter Five, titled Humanitarian Aid and Conflict– An Oxymoron No More," sets the stage for my detour. Spurred by a gentle, yet earth-shattering question posed by a distinguished professor, I was asked if I thought the provision of resources in the form of humanitarian-aid projects ever caused conflict for the people we were trying to help. How could it be that the intended good resulted in conflict? I had failed to ask the deeper questions regarding the intended and unintended positive and negative consequences of the delivered projects. His question, and others that ensued, launched my search for answers.

The humanitarian focal point for me had become *sustainability*, but now it contained another dimension to be addressed–that of conflict or potential conflict. My quest, which began in Chapter Six, led me to academia and ultimately to pursue a doctorate in Conflict Analysis and Resolution. Though demanding, the experience proved priceless and offered me a window to the world. Students from around the globe offered their perspectives and insights to conflict, alternatives, and resolutions within their cultures, which helped me gain greater insight into the beneficiaries' viewpoint about humanitarian-aid projects.

Chapter Seven, "Returning to the Field–As an Observer," details the capstone effort of the doctoral program, which is conducting research under the rigors of committee oversight and ultimate acceptance or not. My research led me back to the villages and remote areas in South America, but this time to observe and evaluate ten ongoing projects in terms of sustainability and stakeholder involvement. I captured and recorded a sufficient amount of data that would permit me to complete a defendable analysis, but more importantly to help find a better way to achieve sustainable projects. Reluctantly, I accepted the fact that the only resources I brought to the field were my questions, a curious mind, and a patient ear. From these restraints arose an absolute fact: there is dignity in asking questions and allowing another person to speak.

Part II concludes with Chapter Eight, "Findings and Discoveries." Having gathered the necessary data and information, a lengthy and time-consuming process of analysis was completed. A brief summary of the findings is presented and among those findings is the fact that there are specific steps and systems that can enhance the likelihood of achieving a sustainable outcome. One of those steps is the early and continued involvement of the intended beneficiaries. Ultimately, each project and culture has unique circumstances that require vision, patience, flexibility, mutual understanding, and collaboration.

*"Every path to a new understanding
begins with confusion."*

MASON COOLEY

CHAPTER FIVE

# HUMANITARIAN AID AND CONFLICT—AN OXYMORON NO MORE

## THE PATH TO SUSTAINABILITY TAKES A DETOUR

The years I spent in the field working on humanitarian-aid projects yielded a virtual library of lessons learned—so many that I had a foundation to draw upon anytime a new project was up for consideration or an existing project was evaluated. The lessons on how to implement sustainable projects came together and were always forefront as I sought implementing systems that would best deliver a sustainable impact.

As a part of my never-ending pursuit of funding for projects, I shared the stories and lessons learned, as well as the critical need for sustainable projects with service clubs. Service club members and other private donors responded with both donations and an interest in better understanding the impact of their contributions. A byproduct of my field-driven lessons learned was a new sense of calm. I was now able to look at projects more objectively. Through an objective lens, I saw and realized that working toward sustainable projects brought about dignity and personal growth for the beneficiaries as well as a lessening of the endless dependence of the cycle of donor funding. I felt a new confidence in my fundraising efforts, enhanced by a better understanding. Finally I understood it was the beneficiaries who needed to feel the sense of accomplishment and take pride in the success of projects. I was happy with my personal growth. Certainly there would be refinements to my skills along the way, but surely there would be no more surprises for me.

I had just completed a presentation to a service club as part of a new fundraising effort to drill a much-needed water well in a poor, remote Asian village. Collecting and transporting water for family and community was the women and children's task. The women walked in groups, accompanied by toddlers and children old enough to walk, as well as their infants in hand-woven slings on their backs. The group was comprised of young girls, elderly, and pregnant women. Sometimes women gave birth on the daily trek and continued on their way after the child was delivered. They did all this while carrying five-gallon containers or heavy pottered jugs on their heads over a rocky, uncertain path—village to the stream and back—taking an excess of three hours. The drilling of a water well would relieve the women of this demanding and difficult task, and it was with compassion for these women that I stood before my fellow service club members asking for their support.

Although I had not visited the village, I had been asked by a fellow service club member to make the plea for donations. It seemed important and worthwhile to be the voice for those who could not speak for themselves; however my experience made me cognizant of the fact that the job would not be as simple as bringing a well to the village. Villagers would have to be trained in the upkeep and maintenance of the well, there would have to be access to and availability of replacement parts. Without these components, the well would suffer the fate of so many well-intentioned projects: becoming unusable as soon as one of the parts failed or necessary maintenance was not performed. It was not uncommon to see broken, rusted equipment in the fields, oftentimes due to a lack of planning by the donors. I was concerned. How could we ensure that whatever we did, the good intentions would not end in just another contribution to the already littered field of botched projects?

Living in a country where water is available at the turn of a faucet, service club members were humbled at the thought of the daily struggle of these impoverished and often malnourished women. As part of the presentation, our committee placed five-gallon jugs filled with water around the room. Service club members were challenged to lift them, place them on their heads, and walk around the room. Then they were asked to imagine doing this every day, three hours a day. No one took up the challenge, but the filled water jugs made the point, and funding for the water well was provided that day.

> How could we ensure ... the good intentions would not end in just another contribution to the already littered field of botched projects?

## MEETING THE PROFESSOR

Following the presentation and at the end of the club meeting, several members approached me to express their thanks and share how good they felt about being a part of making the village water well a reality. We shared and bonded in the pride of helping women in a faraway village. Then I was introduced to a gentleman with a different perspective: an accomplished professor from one of Michigan's prestigious state universities who had initiated this fundraising effort. I was honored to meet him in person. After exchanging cordial greetings and briefly discussing the water-well project, the professor asked in a polite and nonthreatening manner, "Do you think the provision of resources in the form of humanitarian-aid projects ever causes conflict for the people you are trying to help?"

Quite frankly, I was startled by his question and had never really given thought to humanitarian-aid projects causing conflict. My gut response was a quick, "No!"

The question seemed particularly peculiar since the professor had brought the project to the service club. But I soon learned that he had been born and raised in the impoverished country where the water well was destined; in fact, his parents and other family members still lived there. Certainly he thought the drilling of a water well was a good idea, or he wouldn't have initiated the project.

"Would this new water well have caused conflict in the village where you lived as a child?" I asked.

"It very likely could have," said the professor, "had they not thought about and prepared for a resource that they never had access to in the past—water." The professor told me that in his native culture, as in many cultures, it was the work/job of women to provide water for the family. Along with gathering the water, the trip to and from the river provided social time for the women and children; it permitted them to wash the family laundry—often accomplished by pounding and rubbing the clothing on their favorite smooth rock in the stream; some of these rocks had been used by multiple generations. They also bathed themselves and their children. "Yes," the professor agreed, "it is a long, laborious trip for the women and children and the work is tedious, but it is a task that gives women status in their village community; it brought value and personal dignity to the family through the skilled performance of this chore.

"Consider this hypothetical," suggested the professor. "Suppose the kind- and big-hearted members of our service club provided the financial resources for a water well to be drilled in this designated village. Heroically we were rescuing the women and children from the daily, incredibly hard labor of carrying water on their heads for three hours each day. Due to our generosity, there would no longer be the requirement or need for the women and children to make the journey. However, the males in the community would no longer rely on the women to provide the water since it is now conveniently located in the village. Might this generous humanitarian act of the service club devalue the significance of the role of women and their contribution toward the well-being of their family and the village community?"

A cascade of unanswered questions followed as we discussed humanitarian aid and conflict; more than an hour passed and my questions continued. I was waking up—very much like the awareness I experienced years earlier regarding the significance of sustainability in projects.

If there were no *pro-active planning* for the provision of this resource to the community, how would the residents of the village determine the most important use of the water, or the equitable distribution of the water, and address other issues that arose? How would this new community resource change the complexion and culture of the village? What would the women do with the three extra hours a day? When and where would the women and children gather to socialize, support one another, and pass to each succeeding generation the cultural cohesiveness that was brought about by the daily trek for water? Would the women now be devalued in the community since they would be contributing less to the physical well-being of the family? And a water well has limits; so how much water could be used by each family and for what purposes? Should the water from the well be used for commercial purposes and the women still transport water that is used for personal family use? Should the water be used for economic community development through

> **The answers must come about through proper planning and in a proactive manner with all stakeholders having a voice.**

agricultural or livestock undertakings? Who would make these decisions? How would these decisions be made?

The professor helped me understand that there are answers to these questions and others, but the answers must come about through proper planning and in a proactive manner with all stakeholders having a voice. He explained that some villages faced with the water-well situation decided on a personal tax, a "user tax" so to speak. If the village residents wanted to use it for personal economic development by beginning an agricultural project, or use it for livestock, maybe they would pay an additional amount beyond the personal family usage of water. Many of the villages had no currency and had traditionally bartered for the exchange of goods, so water-well usage transaction modes would need to be developed. I could not help but wonder if perhaps it were these types of situations that gave birth to bureaucracies and the need for public policy.

The professor had initiated a university-centered program in response to a similar water-well project, where the women encountered a void in their day due to the installation of a nearby well. Using university students in a study-abroad scenario, the professor's program provided literacy tutoring for the women during the time that was normally reserved for carrying water. The women and children, who were being taught by the university interns, were learning to read and write. Acquiring this knowledge opened their lives to the possibility of a future never before possible. So in this case, the installation of the water well ultimately empowered the women with skills leading toward self-determination—an unintended positive consequence.

At the end of our conversation, the professor and I exchanged business cards and promises of future communications on the subject of humanitarian-aid projects and conflict. However, the topic of discussion and the new questions raised during our conversation weighed heavily on my mind the rest of that day and for many days thereafter. In my zest to help those less fortunate, I had failed to ask the deeper questions regarding the intended and unintended positive and negative consequences of the delivered projects. I'd never even imagined that our good intentions might cause conflict within the village community.

Mentally, I reviewed the aid projects that the service club had been involved in over the last ten years—some that I had fervently spearheaded. Was it possible that our good intentions had brought *conflict* to the communities? We had acknowledged and addressed the negativity of causing dependency on donors and the non-sustainability of projects, but now my personal understanding of projects was getting broader and deeper. How could we ensure that proactive steps were taken to prevent conflict due to humanitarian aid? Or, if it was already present in a project, how could conflict be dealt with most effectively and constructively? It has always been troublesome for me to realize that I don't even know what I don't know!

To find answers, I was ultimately led down a new and unexpected path into the halls of academia. Initially, I thought this would be a relatively brief and simple jaunt—just do some research regarding the unintended consequences of humanitarian aid. But I found no definitive answers to my questions and subsequently spent the next five years in studies and research, seeking them.

In the course of this effort, I came to fully understand that the professor's initial question would be just as life changing as was Nyoman's question poised to me on the edge of the rice field many years ago.

Just as I found the answer to Nyoman's question through taking action, I was drawn to action in response to the professor's question—although it would not be as simple as buying a water buffalo.

*"Education is not the filling of a pail,
but the lighting of a fire."*

WILLIAM BUTLER YEATS

CHAPTER SIX

# SEARCHING FOR ANSWERS

## GOING BACK TO SCHOOL

Academia, with its challenges and rewards, has always had a special appeal for me; I consider myself a lifelong learner and am naturally curious. Searching in the library or on the Internet for the latest information on any given subject was a zone I traveled comfortably. The conversation with the professor and his question regarding the relationship of conflict to humanitarian-aid projects shook my confidence. Finding no answers from my field experience, and unsatisfied with the answers in the current research, there remained a gap in my knowledge and efforts toward sustainable projects. How many other voids were there that I was not even aware of, and was I promoting projects that brought conflict to communities? To satisfy my need to know and to help improve the delivery of sustainable humanitarian-aid projects, I toyed with the idea of returning to school for a Ph.D.

I had a bachelor's degree in psychology and a master's

degree in clinical psychology, with a limited license to practice clinical psychology. For seventeen years the field of psychology was my passion and my livelihood. Helping people find the pieces to the puzzles in their lives and identify the formulas that led toward personal balance and skills in problem solving was intellectually and emotionally stimulating.

Later in life, I returned to school to learn about the business world, acquiring an MBA, and spent the next ten years consulting with companies in the areas of leadership, change management, and executive-communication skills. The area of business was of growing interest to me; just as in clinical psychology, I could see the positive and negative impact an individual's employment could have on his or her personal life and relationships. Organizations are a microcosm of the larger world, and interactions within that structure are similar to the relationships within a family; many of the same pieces of the puzzle and problem-solving skills applied. It was interesting to see skills relate to both the personal and professional lives of clients.

Knowledge learned and skills acquired in each of these professions were invaluable, as my participation in humanitarian-aid projects evolved. Aside from my family, humanitarian-aid projects were my greatest passion. I wanted to leave no stone unturned in pursuing the development of grassroots, sustainable, humanitarian projects. I just wasn't prepared to return to a college campus.

At the tender age of fifty-two, did it make sense to pursue a Ph.D.? If I had searched near and far, I doubt I would have found a career counselor or life coach who would have encouraged me to travel the academic road once again to find the answers to the ever-present, ever-deepening, and ever-increasing questions regarding conflict and the unintended consequences of humanitarian-aid projects. But, I tend to be a bit unconventional in my thoughts and behavior, and I could feel myself drawing ever closer to the pursuit. Excited by the potential for a deeper understanding, I was unwilling to stop myself.

As I researched the few doctoral programs related to this area of study, my thirst for answers intensified—particularly as it became clear that others were pursuing the same knowledge about conflict, and the causes and the means for successful resolution. Most of us understand that conflict is a natural occurrence in life and neither avoidance nor denial is effective methods of getting around it. Conflict has a positive side to it and if it were to be ever-present in project management, how could we make it work to our best advantage? It was also affirming to know my fellow searchers/learners were asking my questions from several different perspectives and disciplines—including anthropology, business, psychology, political science, and economics. Despite my age, despite the cost, and despite the hardships that would follow, it soon became clear that returning to school—one more time—would be the best way for me to methodically gain the knowledge and information. Seeking to understand the current research, and contribute, through additional research, toward the understanding of how providing aid had the potential to create conflict for the beneficiaries seemed my destiny.

## Selecting the Right Academic Program

When the search for the right academic program was completed, I was both challenged by my selection and excited about its potential. If accepted into the program, I was going to pursue a doctorate degree in Conflict Analysis and Resolution. There was the detailed, sometimes tedious, application process, and finally a personal interview with the doctoral committee. They wanted to hear the voice of perspective students regarding commitment, goals, and objectives, and the timeline to complete the program.

A university in Southern Florida, Nova Southeastern University, some distance from my Northern Michigan home, offered the program I pursued. It is a hybrid program that combines online learning and a mandatory residential component—the best of both worlds since I didn't have to relocate and I would still have the opportunity, in fact, requirement, to periodically interact face-to-face with the other students and professors. It is imperative for me to actually see people, have in-person discussions, and read body language, as well as give and get energy from others who are eager to grow in a learning environment.

The portion of the program that required students to be on campus is referred to as the Residential Institute (RI). Though intensive with packed schedules, the RI sessions produced some of my greatest and most treasured experiences. Living and learning with people from diverse cultures (students and faculty represented more than fifteen countries and regions of the world, including many countries in Africa, Europe, and the Caribbean) in an academic environment was exhilarating and meaningful. RI afforded me the chance to have formal and informal conversations with fellow world citizens regarding our passions surrounding conflict and appropriate steps toward positive, peaceful resolution. Our knowledge and understanding expanded when we took in another's perspective on conflict within our cultures, and I gained greater insight into the aid beneficiaries' viewpoint about humanitarian-aid projects. And, as my life grew richer, I was propelled to dig deeper.

I went from feeling and thinking that "completing the

required coursework would take forever" to "I can't believe I am finally finished." After weeks of late-night studying and reviewing endless class notes, I passed my qualifying exam. But, there was still one final hurdle.

## PREPARING FOR THE RESEARCH

A Ph.D. program traditionally requires that each doctoral candidate conduct original, independent research that will contribute to a greater body of knowledge. The process begins with formulating a research question, often centered on the factors of how, what, or why something occurs or exists. While the concept of creating one's research question seems straightforward, the reality is that the research question—formulated with the precision to make it past the doctoral committee and the defense of the dissertation proposal—is often elusive and the cause of many sleepless nights. While the general topic surrounding my yet-to-be-finalized research question was solidly rooted in my mind—the matter of humanitarian-development aid projects causing conflict—the actual question eluded me. It was only after stepping back and examining my humanitarian-aid project roots that I was able to develop my research question.

My time in the field, supporting and spearheading projects, spanned more than a decade. I had volunteered as only one of thousands in Rotary International, a service organization whose membership consists of 1.2 million active community leaders and professionals from 160 countries; all bonded together by the motto of *Service Above Self*. Collectively, whether through donations from home or being present in the field, there are thousands of people from many sources and nations seeking to improve the lives of those less fortunate. They are from various volunteer organizations, church groups, service clubs, nonprofit organizations, the Peace Corps, non-governmental offices (NGOs), etc. Often I was reminded of how hard so many people were working on the behalf of others; it was humbling to witness their sacrifices and level of dedication. Each of us, with the best of intentions, sought to help others who were less fortunate.

As I recalled the variety of projects I had been involved with, witnessed, or saw the results of, questions began to circulate in my mind: Is the aid really helpful and effective? If not, why? Is there a possibility that the aid is actually causing harm to the people we are attempting to help? Have the donations and volunteer hours been effective at igniting change, leading toward a more equitable world? Are the methods currently being used sustainable? The answers to these questions are important for me, and it seemed as though they would be equally important to the thousands of people seeking to help through the support of projects. Didn't we all want to know if our efforts mattered or caused harm? Now, I had a group of questions that essentially centered on the same topic, but I still needed to narrow them down to one— one question that could be answered through my research, contributing to a greater body of knowledge in my field, and ultimately leading to the defense of a dissertation.

Using the group of questions as a general guide, I turned my thoughts to what I'd learned in the classroom, and it didn't take long to focus on negotiation. The theory and practice of negotiation is primary in our academic program of conflict analysis and resolution. If humanitarian-aid projects potentially caused conflict among the beneficiaries, negotiation may serve as a valuable tool in a proactive approach to address conflict. I had questions formulated from reflecting on my time in the field, plus negotiation as an integral tool to deal with issue conflict, leaving one missing piece to a final research question that would respond to my questions. That piece was sustainability.

While my introduction to sustainability was rooted in the interaction with Nyoman, sustainability has become a global mantra for desired outcomes, whether for businesses or community-development projects. Sustainability embraces the economic, environmental, cultural, and social aspects of efforts. Could the act of integrative negotiation between major stakeholders enhance the potential for the sustainability of projects and decrease possible conflict? Finally, the research question and even the methodology to investigate this matter were becoming clear. My research question became: What is the relationship between negotiation and sustainability in humanitarian-development aid projects? In other words, did the process of integrative negotiation incorporated into efforts of achieving sustainability in humanitarian-aid projects have a positive or negative effect in reducing or eliminating conflict?

## Conducting the Research[*]

The design of my research, successfully defended as part of the overall dissertation proposal, outlined the strategy that would be used to examine a number of nonprofit foundations investing in sustainable community-development projects. All of the field research, consisting of the actual observation and evaluation of projects, occurred in impoverished countries in Central America.

Ultimately, ten foundations participated in the research study and, in doing so, agreed to permit me to accomplish the following in accordance with the written research contract:

---

[*]Information presented in this book highlights certain details from the actual dissertation and is not intended to represent it in its entirety. Access to the dissertation, with all of its details and references, is detailed in the appendix.

1. Review their record of grant approvals and denials.

2. Conduct a semi-structured interview with the executive director or a member of the board of directors for the foundation with both parties communicating openly and with transparency.

3. Evaluate their randomly selected project(s) taking place in the field.

4. Conduct semi-structured interviews with the field program directors and/or project managers(s) as well as the beneficiaries of the selected projects, and support open communication among all parties.

The specific foundations and projects participating in the research remain confidential. It was necessary to protect the identity of the foundations, boards of directors, project managers, and the beneficiaries to ensure candor throughout the investigative process and to guarantee that their donor base would not be influenced negatively or positively as a result of the research. The entire process of interviews and the collection of information led me to develop a great deal of respect and admiration for the interviewees, their receptiveness toward me, their willingness to discuss the projects, and their candor in their descriptions of the strengths and weaknesses of the projects they so diligently watched over.

To ensure there would be no conflict of interest, none of the projects that were observed and evaluated had been supported by my service organization, nor did I have prior involvement with the foundations selected, such as applying for and/or being awarded grants for other projects. None of the ten foundations provided remuneration to me for the evaluations. In an act of goodwill and gratitude for their time and participation, the foundations were given a final copy of the dissertation, along with a title code that allowed them to identify only their foundation—so they could identify the data relating to them as it compared to other projects that were also evaluated.

Following the completion of the structured interviews with the foundation representatives from the board of directors and review of their documentation, which took place stateside, I was finally off to the field to observe and interview project managers, the beneficiaries, and perform the project evaluations. The ten identified projects fell under the umbrella of sustainable, economic community development and were categorized into three general areas: housing projects, microfinance, and educational sponsorships.

*"Somewhere, something incredible
is waiting to be known."*

CARL SAGAN

CHAPTER SEVEN

# RETURNING TO THE FIELD —AS AN OBSERVER

## MAKING THE TRANSITION

While it felt wonderful to return to the field, the experience was unfamiliar—very different from more than a decade of humanitarian-aid-project experience. I was now in the field as an objective researcher to observe and evaluate projects. At first, it was quite awkward and unsettling for me to observe and listen to those in need without offering solutions or help or opinions; I was no longer a "fixer." This new role required serious self-discipline.

As I battled my chronic desire to fix the problem, I often thought of my field experiences in Indonesia: being led by my heart and working to send a village of children to school. Those times produced a more dignified feeling because I believed I was there to lend a hand and help, to bring whatever resources I could to the cause. Standing back and observing felt as though I were being indifferent, uncaring; perhaps insensitive. As an objective researcher, I was helpless to change the situation. To handle this new role, I needed to remind myself of the dependency and maybe even unnecessary conflict caused by previous projects for past beneficiaries and remember that I was now in search of better methods.

But there were also some advantages to spending time in the field as an objective researcher. It forced me to sharpen my listening skills and develop an ability to observe with friendliness, warmth, and openness. It increased the quality time I was spending with project managers and the beneficiaries, gaining a deeper understanding of the culture as well as a different perspective on the projects.

In doing this research, I was no longer practicing the Western-style problem-solving method of riding in on a white horse and galloping quickly through the village to assess the situation. Now, my goal was to take time and give beneficiaries the utmost respect and to solicit from them, if they chose to interact with me, answers to a number of straightforward questions. Through translators, I repeatedly asked:

- ◆ Is there a problem? (For instance, a lack of resources that, if supplied, might bring the opportunity for them to solve the problem.)

- ◆ If so, what do they consider the problem and why is it a problem?

- ◆ What are their ideas about a solution to the problem they identified?

- ◆ What have they already done to try to solve the problem? What was successful, what was not, and why?

- ◆ What are they willing to do to contribute toward the solution of the stated problem?

◆ What would they consider helpful from an outsider, if anything?

◆ What resource, if made available, would be most beneficial to the community?

◆ What resource, if made available to the individual, would be most beneficial?

◆ How would the provision of this resource benefit the community?

◆ What are the possible conflicts that may occur within the community or culture if this change occurred?

◆ How would the community address or resolve this conflict?

◆ Could the community do anything to keep this conflict from occurring?

◆ How would the community sustain the benefits of this resource?

In the past, these questions may never have been asked of the beneficiaries. I must admit that the act of asking at least five "why" questions and then waiting while the beneficiaries reflected required me to increase my level of patience. Initially I wasn't sure why this was so difficult or foreign to me; after all, I practiced patience all the time at home. It was awkward and uncomfortable to recognize that I had never really considered these questions to be important; now they seemed to be the only important questions. Previously, if a child was suffering physical symptoms of malnutrition, the reasons why, as well as the solutions, seemed obvious to others and myself—the outsiders—so asking the "why" questions seemed absurd. It was much more satisfying to take action: obtain food for the hungry, provide clean water via water filters or drilling a water well, or raise money for educational scholarships. Whatever the problem, "we" had the solution. It took me years to realize none of the solutions to what I perceived as the problem were really that simple. More importantly, whatever "we" thought the problem was did not matter until the people living in that situation thought it was a problem; the same with the solutions to the problem.

During my time in the field as a researcher, I had periods of self-reflection and discovery. I thought back to years earlier, to my days of studying in the MBA program, to teaching organizational behavior, and to my clinical psychology practice. In all of these settings it was understood that you should not assume to know what the organizational or personal problems are or what the solutions might be. We learned the skill of framing and asking what people perceived the problem to be; we were trained to listen to responses and encourage appropriate steps to resolve the problem. We were taught to ask for suggestions for solutions. There is dignity to asking a question and allowing another person to speak. Why had it been so difficult to apply that simple principle to these projects? It took Nyoman, the impoverished Indonesian rice farmer, to awaken me to the fact that he could provide for his own children—if asked a few simple questions and then provided an opportunity. And I hadn't even had the good sense to ask the question. Nyoman had to hand it to me. How grateful I am that Nyoman had the courage to step forward and teach me that important lesson.

> Whatever "we" thought the problem was did not matter until the people living in that situation thought it was a problem ...

As the research progressed, I began to accept the fact that the only resources I brought to the field were my questions, a curious mind, and a patient ear. With strength and conviction, I clung to the hope that this research would ultimately help bring a deeper understanding and therefore influence systems of giving and delivering humanitarian-aid projects in community development. I forged ahead with objectivity, temporarily suspending my craving to provide tangible resources for people in need. Research data was collected and certain other discoveries made.

## SUSTAINABILITY MEANS WHAT?

The stated objective of all the projects being observed and evaluated during my research was "sustainable community development through the use of integrative negotiation among major stakeholders." All of the interviews with members of the various boards of directors that took place stateside confirmed this objective. In my mind, the issue of sustainability was set—that is until I began to interview the project managers in the field. Each project manager interpreted steps toward sustainability as well as an integrative negotiation with major stakeholders according to his or her understanding of needs and circumstances. Sustainability was a key component to their stated objectives, yet there was not a common understanding of the term. Its use and definition varied among the representatives of the boards of directors that had been interviewed, the foundations' written documents stating their goals and objectives, the project managers, and me—the researcher. This significant issue did not fully surface until I was in the field conducting interviews with project managers. Minimally, it proved to be a point of frustration for all of us, but my biggest fear was that it augured a flaw in the research design.

Preparing for the research, I knew that experts in different disciplines—such as anthropologists, economists, and environmentalists—viewed sustainability through different lenses, but I mistakenly and naïvely assumed that all people involved in humanitarian-aid projects would share a common understanding of the definition of sustainability within our projects. I learned a valuable lesson: even within our own fields of interest, it is critical that we all view key terms with a common understanding, and it is the responsibility of each of us to ensure this common understanding is achieved. This lesson holds true whether we are talking with our family members, conversations within business organizations, educational settings, political groups, church groups, etc. How many times have we found ourselves in disagreement or conflict with someone, only to later learn that we probably did agree on the essential elements of the area of concern, but we were stating the same thing in different words?

Fourteen project managers representing the various projects I was evaluating participated in semi-structured interviews. These project managers were at the helm of projects intended for sustainable community development, and the projects fell into three general categories: the provision of housing for impoverished families, microloans for entrepreneurs, and providing educational sponsorships for children. Patterns and clusters of information began to emerge as the field interviews took place. For instance, the project managers of housing projects responded generally that sustainability of the project would depend on "if it could hold the interest of current and potential future donors; if so, it would continue to generate funds." In other words, even if the project and its beneficiaries remained dependent on external resources for survival—including the time of a salaried professional project manager, staff and/or volunteers, talent of outside consultants, and the financial resources generated by the nonprofit organization—the project would be considered sustainable. This definition of *sustainability* did not fall into alignment with any I had seen in the literature and was not consistent with definitions found in other disciplines.

Conversely, the microloan project managers stated that a project was sustainable when the microloan is repaid with the assigned interest and the beneficiary is now economically self-sustaining and no longer dependent on funding from donors. The traditional microloan model used allows the NGO to continually revolve funds: as each loan with interest is repaid, a new loan may be generated. One of the goals of the microloan organization is to increase the number/volume of borrowers, create efficiency through systems, and use the interest generated to pay the project's administrative costs. This formula increases the likelihood that the NGO will become self-sustaining and the beneficiary/entrepreneur will also become economically independent, thereby, eventually creating no long-term dependence for the beneficiaries on the donors.

> The NGO will become self-sustaining and the beneficiary/ entrepreneur will also become economically independent ...

Finally, the project managers of the educational sponsorship projects considered that the sustainability of the projects was reliant on the actions of future generations. The current generation was receiving an education through the project and would then be better prepared for the future. Although the donors were responding to the needs of the current generation for an education, the assumption was that future generations would be provided the resources for an education by this current generation, and they would no longer be dependent on outside financial resources.

The term *sustainability* held different meaning for each project manager. One entity believed their project was sustainable even if there was long-term dependence of the beneficiary on the resources of the nonprofit organization. The very foundation/sustainability of the program was built on maintaining the interest of long-term donors; the program manager felt this was appropriate since they had a twenty-year history successfully attracting funds. Conversely there were microloan programs that considered a project sustainable if the beneficiary became economically self-reliant by generating his or her own money through entrepreneurship. The educational sponsorship project was intentionally designed to build sustainability by allowing the future generation to be dependent on the generosity of the current generation.

As my interviews with the project managers were coming to an end, it was abundantly clear that the term *sustainability* needed an agreed-upon definition.

## Knowing the Stakeholders

While in the field, I also discovered less than unanimous viewpoints on the identification of stakeholders. After the sustainability debacle, it was—in the immortal words of Yogi Berra—"like déjà vu all over again." During the interviews that occurred stateside with representatives of the boards of directors of the various foundations, I was told that they did indeed utilize the process of integrative negotiation with major stakeholders to identify the problem and determine the solution through potential projects. However, in the process of interviewing the project managers and beneficiaries, it became apparent that there was no consistent agreement or shared understanding on the identification of the major stakeholders in a project. Without that agreement, how could I determine if the process of integrative negotiation had occurred? This was another challenge to the research.

In the field, many of the projects considered the major stakeholders to be the donors—such as large foundations and grant providers—and the implementing NGO. The negotiations for all project ideas/concept, planning, and budgets took place between the two stakeholders: donors and the implementing nonprofit organization. The end-user of the project, the beneficiary, was rarely included in the negotiation process and was not represented by either party in the negotiations. As such, the beneficiaries did not have a voice in the identification of the problem, the solution, or desired outcome; they were not considered stakeholders. The following drawing illustrates what was taking place.

## Negotiations With Stakeholders

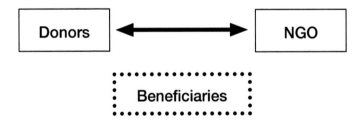

According to some project managers, the specific beneficiary (e.g., recipient in a housing project) oftentimes was not identified in the beginning stages of the project-management cycle. The nonprofit organization or the donor(s) identified the problem (e.g., impoverished homeless people), the solution, (e.g., build houses), and gathered potential resources to address the problem. Using that formula, it would have been impossible to include the beneficiary in the concept or planning stages of the project. This omission of housing beneficiaries as stakeholders was confirmed during twenty-five interviews with beneficiaries, who rarely identified themselves as major stakeholders with the ability to negotiate desired outcomes in a project.

In contrast to the housing projects, the microloan and education projects did incorporate the beneficiaries as major stakeholders, and they participated in the process of integrative negotiation at the start of the project. The strong and committed voice of the beneficiaries was considered a key component to the overall project—a voice to be heard in the quest to ensure economic self-sustainability as well as to eliminate the potential harm of long-term dependency on donors. Again, this was confirmed in twenty interviews with the microloan beneficiaries conducted in the field. The following drawing illustrates what was taking place.

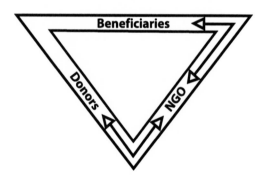

## WORKING WITH TRANSLATORS— BRINGING TWO WORLDS TOGETHER

Much to my chagrin, even after four years of high-school Latin, I speak only English. The role of the translator in this field research was paramount to its success, and conducting interviews through the translators took time and patience. Many of the interviews with beneficiaries were conducted in different dialects. There were times when interviews required two different skilled translators: one to translate from English to the language in that country and then another to translate and interpret in a specific dialect. The "why" questions that I'd constructed for the research seemed simple enough before going into the field, but after only a few interviews, the questions quickly became more and more basic. One question often led to many more, but this approach gave the beneficiary the opportunity to express ideas, solutions, and thoughts on what may never have been asked or voiced in the past. In addition, the process of interviewing through a translator gave me a greater opportunity to listen and hear what beneficiaries had to say.

The use of a translator seemed to triple the time needed to accomplish an interview, not just because of the translation process, but also because of time needed to understand and convey the true intent of what was said. There were times when I knew that my question was not being translated properly to the beneficiary. Certainly, this was not deliberate; perhaps the translator did not fully understand the question or there may have been a problem with the vocabulary or concepts. All interviews were tape-recorded, but because of the time it took to weave the conversation through the translators, I was able to take detailed notes as well as photos of the surroundings and those observing us. Sometimes the observers would join the conversation.

I had overestimated how many interviews could be accomplished in a day. I learned how to phrase the questions and I paused as long as necessary for responses that would indicate that both the translator and the beneficiary had understood my questions and, equally important, that I understood the responses. It was a critical and tedious process. Due to my Western-derived impatience, in the beginning I was tempted to rush. But, with less than two interviews completed, I began to realize that persistence and fortitude would bring much richer content, and the quality of the interview was more important than a daily quantity completed.

Depending on my country location and the dialect being spoken by the residents, there were several different translators. One interview took me deep into a rural area with a reluctant translator. It was his first day with me, and we would spend three days together so it was important that we go through the basic process of understanding and accommodating each other's needs for food, water, breaks, and shelter at the end of the day. It also took time to be certain we had a common understanding of the process and goal of the interviews, and it was critical that the translator tell me exactly what the interviewee was saying even if it seemed rude or out of context to him. All of the translators were working independently and had been contacted by an NGO not involved in the project being evaluated. The foundations involved in the research usually offered a translator; however, in my desire to preserve objectivity, I declined. I did not want to risk a conflict of interest and a need to focus on the most positive or successful aspects of the project influencing the responses of the interviewee. However, the disadvantage of contracting objective translators was that they rarely understood the concept of humanitarian aid or the specific vocabulary, and they may have also been biased about the topic. The people I contracted were not always professional translators and were frequently hired because of their availability and proximity to the interview site. They were almost always confused about why a woman, probably a mother and grandmother from the West, was traveling to their country asking questions of poor people. Why wasn't I at home taking care of my family?

*"Research is to see what everybody else has seen,*
*and to think what nobody else has thought."*
ALBERT SZENT-GYORGYI

CHAPTER EIGHT

# FINDINGS AND DISCOVERIES

Over the past decade, I'd gleaned a deeper understanding of projects and the benefits of donor contributions each time I returned home from the field. This trip was no different, but this time my understanding came from objective research. During this plane ride home I thought not about how I'd gather resources to be sent into the field, but rather how to begin untangling the precious data. Throughout the process of coding and interpreting the data, I was indeed thankful for the cooperation of project managers and beneficiaries. We had a predetermined structural method to identify what I had witnessed and subsequently place it in categories. This procedure would help lead to conclusions and meaning.

Analysis of data can be a long, arduous process. It requires listening to the tapes over and over, coding the information, and then framing the emerging information into findings. At the end of the process, significant findings are identified and incorporated into the dissertation. The following sections highlight just a few of my findings and discoveries.

## When the Theory of Sustainability Meets Reality

The number-one discovery was the recognition that there is no single method of guaranteeing a sustainable humanitarian project. No one-size-fits-all solution. No universal application of sustainability. But there are specific steps and systems that can enhance the likelihood of achieving a sustainable outcome. Many NGOs develop projects with the fervent hope and desire of designing a project that is sustainable, addresses or solves a specific problem, and can be duplicated throughout the world. There was a time when I shared that goal and would try to visualize solutions that would bring peace to the world; how amazing it would be to design the perfect, comprehensive program that could solve the problem of poverty and ultimately contribute toward a nonviolent world. However, now I have come to understand that each culture, community, village, neighborhood, and person deserves the recognition that they are unique. Every person is capable of, and deserves the opportunity to develop solutions to his or her own self-identified problems.

## Discovering a Path Forward Through Integrative Negotiation

It was discovered during the field research that when the beneficiaries did develop the behavioral and communication skills needed to participate in collective choice, these skills then transferred to the process of negotiation. Beneficiaries, as group members, were then better able to represent themselves by identifying their needs and wants. Conversely, when the project manager neither negotiated with the beneficiaries nor ensured that they were adequately represented in the project-management cycle, the recipients of aid were less successful at negotiations.

An overall finding of this study showed the contributions of integrative negotiation outcomes included:

1. When all interested parties are involved in the process of collaborative decision making through the process of integrative negotiation, there is an increased likelihood of producing a sustainable outcome.

2. When the process of integrative negotiation with the beneficiaries identified as major stakeholders occurs at each stage of the project-management cycle, there is a greater likelihood of a sustainable outcome.

3. When beneficiaries are involved in the negotiation process, they gain additional communication and collective decision-making skills that are transferable to resolving conflict—from community disputes to conflicts within families.

When integrative negotiation is practiced between the parties, the process itself is respectful of all parties, as it requires cooperation and mutual understanding. In addition, the process acknowledges the beneficiaries' right to self-governance, self-determination, and cultural integrity. Interviews with the beneficiaries revealed that they want to have an integral, meaningful voice and role in the decision-making process regarding opportunities that will impact their future and that of their children.

## Collective Decision Making
## Versus Individual Self-Interest

The complex variables involved in collective choice are challenging even in the best of circumstances. This was especially true in an endeavor to create a new sustainable community of houses that was observed during my objective field research. The impoverished people living on the periphery of the city dump struggle for daily survival. They were not, and most likely never had been, part of a greater functional community. When these individuals were selected to be the recipients of housing in a new community, social dynamics changed abruptly. They did not know each other, did not possess community social skills, and met for the first time as they began their community interaction by building new homes. Their sweat equity was a down payment on their home. Side by side they sweated with the very people that they competed with daily for resources at the city dump, and they were expected to cooperate and collaborate in a collective decision-making process to accomplish the building of a new community. This often required special training—new skills and techniques, group cooperation, and team building.

The project research determined that it had not been realistic to expect that the individual family survival skills born in the practice of self-interest would easily transfer and be successful in a model that required people to make decisions based on the greater good, interest, and needs of the community, with the anticipation of building sustainability through collective choice—all without training—practically ensuring discontent and a less-than-positive outcome to the project.

## Boiling It Down to the Essentials

Near the end of the research process for identifying the findings and discoveries, I felt a great reluctance to put away the notes and tapes, to stop coding the information, to say "enough." It seemed as if there was always another aspect of data to examine or another outcome to discover, but reluctantly I finally concluded my research. Then I reflected on what I had learned, and I had learned a great deal.

Each project and culture has unique circumstances that require vision, patience, flexibility, mutual understanding, collaboration, and oftentimes placing collective needs, rights, and interests above individual interests. This is no easy task. While there is still no concrete procedure applicable to all situations, there are commonalities and lessons that can be adapted in each project to increase the likelihood of a sustainable outcome. They are:

1. At all times it is imperative to be aware and respectful of local culture and knowledge.

2. Educational/informational training in collaborative decision making and integrative negotiation skills for the stakeholders that incorporates local knowledge and is culturally appropriate will most likely expedite the process of onsite negotiation.

3. There is substantial evidence that the beneficiaries often lacked an understanding of the project objectives or of the process that would occur to reach a sustainable outcome. Information is power, so it is essential that beneficiaries, as recognized stakeholders, assist in the formulation of project objectives.

4. Training in the skill of integrative negotiation has the potential to proactively resolve conflict and decrease inefficiency and ineffective project management; therefore, it is highly recommended that minimally the project managers, and preferably all stakeholders, receive formal training in the process of integrative negotiation. The project managers reported that they negotiate specific areas within the project-management cycle; this may occur with partner NGOs, donors, and/ or beneficiaries.

5. Mindful adherence to the steps of a project-management cycle consisting of: concept/design, planning, implementation, and ongoing evaluation are helpful in that this provides a master plan. A well-thought-out and negotiated master strategic plan may resolve difficulties as they arise.

6. A legitimately negotiated exit strategy is a critical step in the planning stage of the project cycle if the intended impact is sustainability.

7. All NGOs bring with them a mandate or mission; it is imperative that this pre-identified mission be congruent with the needs and interests of the potential beneficiaries. The best way to gain this understanding is to be respectful of the beneficiaries by asking the simple questions stated in Chapter 7.

# PART III

## LESSONS LEARNED, LESSONS SHARED

*"Believe you can and you are halfway there."*
THEODORE ROOSEVELT

*"Never be satisfied with what you achieve, because it all pales in comparison with what you are capable of doing in the future."*

## Introduction

Part III is filled with five chapters of practical and essential lessons, which begins and ends with sustainability. Sandwiched between the two sustainability chapters are relationship building, integrative negotiation, and the four-stage project-management cycle. Sustainability is the logical starting point of consideration in just about everything we do; it is the goal, so it is the endpoint as well. Sustainability, as presented in Chapter Nine, is described in an overview, its vital link to humanitarian aid discussed, and the need to consider sustainability beyond humanitarian aid detailed.

In the case of humanitarian aid, sustainability becomes synonymous with self-sufficiency on the part of the beneficiary. I have experienced the privilege of witnessing the results and rewards brought forth when families living in poverty are given a chance to lift themselves and stand on their own. It is truly incredible; for them, for me, and for the future soundness of humanitarian aid. Likewise, sustainability in an organization, school, or personal effort brings about independency from any recurring drains on scarce resources—be it time, energy, or money.

Relationship building, the second component presented, is about the efforts to successfully transform individuals with different ideas and interests into a united, collective group of stakeholders. When efforts put forth to build relationships are successful, the group or all stakeholders are better able to achieve a clear focus and understanding of the issues at hand and the potential to achieve the desired outcome is greatly improved.

Integrative negotiation is the third component. It presents a systematic approach where the parties share information and collectively search for options, alternatives, and solutions. The intent is to integrate the other parties' needs and preferences with their own in order to achieve a final agreement.

The process of project management, commonly referred to as the project-management cycle, is presented as the fourth component. The traditional approach to project management, which incorporates four stages—idea/concept, planning, execution, and evaluation—is expanded and refined to include relationship building and integrative negotiation.

To conclude Part III, sustainability is described in terms of a system shift from the old to the new with the integration of two vital components: microfinance and social business. When adopted and correctly applied, each is invaluable in the recipients' efforts to achieve sustainability—free to determine their destiny and to do so without the dependency and uncertainty of donations from donors far away.

*"At the most basic level, the key to ending extreme poverty is to enable the poorest of the poor to get their feet on the ladder of development."*

---

CHAPTER NINE

# SUSTAINABILITY— TO KNOW IT IS TO LOVE IT

Sustainability is the highest and most complete form of efficiency. The goal or objective of sustainability imposes on every policy, program, project, or individual effort an explicit commitment to minimize not only its economic costs but also to maximize its political, social, and environmental benefits.

Sustainability or *sustainable development* means different things to different sectors of society or professions; economists define it one way while anthropologists and environmentalists define it another. Even the United Nations offers its own definition for sustainable development. Borrowing common threads from many definitions, I believe that sustainable development (a sustainable project) may be defined as and achieved when:

1. The effort produces the intended positive impact on the targeted population.

2. The effort does not destroy the natural ecosystem or disrupt the socio-cultural equilibrium of the local community.

3. The effort does not jeopardize resources for future generations.

4. The resulting outcome of the effort does not create dependency on donors or perpetuation based on outside intervention.

## SUSTAINABILITY BEYOND HUMANITARIAN AID
### *"Self-sufficiency is the greatest of all wealth."*

EPICURUS

The concept of sustainability has global recognition and application. Whether applied to humanitarian aid or an individual's personal efforts, educational programs in the school, or the world of business, sustainability or sustainable development is needed now to help ensure tomorrow.

Some corporations have begun integrating sustainability into their business models. Sustainability in the business world is defined in terms of its financial, social, and environmental components, which are the three pillars, more frequently referred to as the "triple bottom line (3BL)." In order to be successful in their sustainability efforts, organizations must incorporate a two-pronged approach. They look inward to address, modify, or correct sustainable shortcomings as well as look outward to partner with local communities and government agencies. Through their successful sustainable efforts, businesses are able to make a profit (economic), contribute to the local community (social), and protect the environment.

When the concept of sustainability is introduced into schools or school systems, the path is similar to that of businesses; schools also have a two-pronged approach. Looking inward, schools integrate the concept and practices of sustainability into their curriculums as well as begin practical application of the principles. Schools are now composting and making sustainable-driven decisions regarding food and cleaning supplies. Externally, schools build relationships with the community to both connect what is being learned with what the community is facing and to collaborate in bringing about sustainable solutions or outcomes. Lessons learned in school may well be carried into adulthood and passed to succeeding generations.

Individuals may develop their own personal sustainability plans. While these plans are frequently focused on contributing to eco awareness or environmental sustainability, a much broader scope should be considered; one that touches all aspects of an individual's life. Following the principles or components that define sustainability, an individual is able to establish goals, benchmarks, and outcomes that will result in a lifestyle centered on sustainability. Living this lifestyle takes commitment and while it is a journey that is never completed, it offers the greatest of freedoms to those who seek it.

## TYING THE SUSTAINABILITY
## AND HUMANITARIAN-AID KNOT

*"Give a man a fish and you feed him for a day.*
*Teach a man to fish and you feed him for a lifetime."*
CHINESE PROVERB

Sustainability and humanitarian projects may often go hand-in-hand. Since being the fortuitous recipient of

Nyoman's question, I have learned over and over again the value of sustainable humanitarian projects. Unfortunately, I have also witnessed the disastrous and heartbreaking results when well-intended projects went terribly wrong because they were not guided by the components that define sustainability. Throughout my involvement in humanitarian projects and associated research, there have been too many instances where the fourth component of sustainability (absence of external dependency) was not upheld or even acknowledged. Many NGOs go so far as to reject the fourth component. I have been told, "A project is sustainable if it remains interesting to the NGO's donors and continues to generate funds through donations." This definition of sustainability as the long-term dependency on external funding to maintain a project or program is unique to NGO, nonprofit, philanthropic ideology. Dependency on well-intended, generous donors does not equate to sustainability of a program. The fallacy of this approach is that no one can accurately predict what donors will do in the future. Priorities and the amount of money earmarked for donations change. We have witnessed a current example of this: as the U.S. economy plummeted, so did charitable donations to nonprofit organizations. As the economy began its downward slide the beneficiaries of humanitarian projects both domestically and internationally suffered the most. A program that believed it was sustainable based on a steady track record of annual donations felt the sting as the day of reckoning arrived with a steady drop in donations.

> **Dependency on well-intended, generous donors does not equate to sustainability of a program.**

## SUSTAINABILITY—CHALLENGES AND OUTCOMES

While sustainable projects or outcomes are certainly needed in all walks of life and are achievable, they may also present challenges. The challenges arise due to the often necessary but imprecise nature of the assumptions made regarding the sustainability project components, whether it is the timeline, the impact on future generations, or what methods will be used to ensure the equitable distribution of benefits. Each quantifier of sustainability must be acknowledged and addressed individually—sometimes repeatedly revisited. Just as practiced in for-profit business, factors and conditions that once seemed unwavering can and do also change in aid projects. The time period from inception of a sustainable effort until the process or product is delivered may be set and appear reasonable at the start; yet, funding delays, maneuvering through bureaucratic wickets, and changes in the availability of material all have an impact on the original target date for completion. It is important to recognize that sustainability is the goal and everything associated with it remains fluid and potentially subject to change.

When properly planned and achieved, sustainable projects not only produce their intended positive outcomes (effectiveness) at the least possible economic cost (efficiency), but they also ensure that the resulting benefits are equally distributed among all the possible beneficiaries or stakeholders (equity). Moreover, these projects impose minimum costs on the larger society, on its natural environment, and on future generations. As I learned and now share: "Sustainability—to know it is to love it."

*"To listen well, is as powerful a means
of influence as to talk well, and is essential
to all true conversation."*

CHINESE PROVERB

CHAPTER TEN

# RELATIONSHIP BUILDING

The second lesson shared is the need for and value of relationship building. Though what I now share was largely derived through association with many humanitarian-aid projects, the reality is that relationship building is applicable in so many different venues: psychologists and therapists talk about it, business and commerce talk about it. Every time two or more individuals come together in any sort of collective effort there is a potential for relationship building. Different terms are used to describe the individuals brought together—*parties, stakeholders, partners,* and *beneficiaries*— regardless of the label, each has a role to play, a need to be fulfilled, and a contribution to make. Whether the duration of the relationship is destined to be short-term or long-term, it is essential that the proper effort go into relationship building. Relationships must be nurtured and, when they are, the bonds remain long after the objective is accomplished.

Many times I have interacted with an individual or a small group of individuals, thinking that our paths would cross but once, only to work with them again years later. The efforts put into building relationships bear fruit over and over—often through generations.

Simply stated, the goals of relationship building are to achieve a clear focus and understanding of the issue, strengthen the bonds and collective effort put forth, and improves the chances for achieving the desired outcome. The broad term of relationship building incorporates a few different categories, including coalitions, alliances, and networks. Humanitarian-aid efforts most commonly bring about a *coalition*, which is defined as a relationship formed over specific issues. Alliances come about when various groups and individuals form relationships around a general agreement or goal. The least cohesive relationship is a *network*, which offers some degree of support and connectivity.

## RELATIONSHIP-BUILDING CHALLENGES

*"Connection gives purpose and meaning to our lives."*
BRENE BROWN

The cohesiveness of a relationship faces both internal and external challenges. An external challenge or reluctance to forming a group may be due to the presence of a largely Western-derived psyche or culture that rewards individual accomplishments and efforts. This solo approach should be resisted even though at the time it may seem the most efficient use of our time. Instead, we should reach out to others to form a team or group to address the issue or problem at hand. Reaching out immediately changes the profile from a singular to a collective brainpower effort and assists in correctly identifying the major stakeholders.

Internal challenges to full relationship building may include ensuring all parties or stakeholders are completely integrated into the group. A reluctance to fully share pertinent information and/or a lack of common understanding or agreement in dealing with issues of differences is fertile breeding ground for future conflict. Everyone in the group, regardless of origin or background, needs to be heard. All too often individuals who have great potential to contribute to the effort are silenced early in the process. Local knowledge is critical in a humanitarian-aid project. This knowledge comes best from the recipients or beneficiaries of the effort; yet, their valuable contribution is often overlooked or passed over without due consideration in the name of efficiency. It is essential that the group invest the time to incorporate local knowledge and understand how the project might impact the current culture. The best of intentions by outsiders may not mesh with local customs, cultures, and

> **Local knowledge is critical in a humanitarian-aid project.**

processes for dealing with various community activities. When local knowledge is not taken into consideration, projects are destined to travel an uncertain path that more often than not will lead to a dead end after the donors return home.

As information emerges regarding the roles, needs, and contributions of the participants, it is important that information be shared openly with transparency. Compartmentalizing critical information by sharing it with some members and not others is a sure way to jeopardize the desired outcome. In humanitarian-aid projects, all too often the beneficiaries do not receive important strategies regarding implementation and their perspective is grossly neglected or undervalued. NGOs from wealthy Western countries often project their own needs and solutions onto other societies and cultures without ever including the beneficiary of the aid as a responsible voice in the identified need and impact. Beneficiaries may share alternative solutions that are more conducive to their culture. Leaving out beneficiaries when there is an exchange of information is harmful and condescending. It fails to empower them to advocate for themselves and creates dependency on those with access to financial resources.

Conflict within a group will occur; you can count on it! As presented in Part II, learning that the delivery of humanitarian aid can and at times does cause conflict led me to study, in great detail, the analysis of conflict and how best to resolve it. Communication, understanding, inclusiveness, and relationship building go a long way in taking a proactive approach to preventing conflict. But conflict is also natural and, if seen as constructive, contributes to the strength of a positive outcome. Since the event of a conflict is a given in most circumstances, systems and methods on how to reach resolution can be developed in advance. Before the first issue of conflict arises, it is important to establish the means by which it will be addressed: various cultures have a variety of ways and means leading to resolution, they may involve a show of hands, honoring a consensus, unanimity, or majority voting or a final decision to be determined by tribal or village leaders or the community of elders. Established approaches toward conflict must be respected.

> Leaving out beneficiaries when there is an exchange of information is harmful and condescending.

In the field, negotiation was often used to address matters of conflict. When a multicultural group is determining how best to address matters of conflict, there must be sensitivity to the conflict-resolution practices used by the different cultures. Two examples that I have come across include conflict-resolution outcomes being determined by a group of elders in the village rather than by individuals. In another culture, *face-saving* was an important component of resolution, preventing public shame or embarrassment toward an individual or group in reaching an agreement.

## RELATIONSHIP-BUILDING REWARDS

In the realm of humanitarian aid, relationship building is generally made up of NGOs and beneficiaries, coupled by a sense of unity based on inclusion rather than behaviors resulting in exclusion of concerned parties. This is reflected through the empowerment derived from increased social capital among the beneficiaries. When all voices are heard, when local knowledge is acknowledged and integrated, when information is shared freely and transparently, bonds are strengthened, beneficiaries are empowered, communities are favorably impacted, and relationships are built because hearts, minds, and efforts have been joined. The process of relationship building decreases the number of conflicts that occur and increases the likelihood of the representation and collaboration of all stakeholders.

*"Cooperation is through the conviction that nobody
can get there unless everybody gets there."*

CHAPTER ELEVEN

# NEGOTIATION

Left unexplored and without full understanding, the
practice of negotiation often suffers from a bad rap. It conjures
words and visions of win-lose, playing hardball, aggressive
behavior, or the caricature of a slick used-car salesman.
The lesson learned and now shared is that negotiation is a
valuable tool when applied to humanitarian-aid projects. It
can be so much more than these negative stereotypes, but
it must be fully understood for a couple important reasons.
The first is the fact that negotiation is one of the most
basic of activities through which human beings pursue the
satisfaction of their individual and collective needs. The
second is that negotiation is widely regarded as the best way
to prevent, manage, resolve, and eventually transform social
conflicts into positive, constructive phenomena. Given its
incredible potential, negotiation must surely make its way
into many facets of society and our lives.

My journey of understanding and integrating negotiation into humanitarian-aid projects began in the Guatemala City dump where I first witnessed the success of connecting educational needs of children to the hunger of the families struggling to find food for their family and recyclable goods to sell. The negotiation between the families and the program director was fierce but effective in the long run, both parties achieving their goals. Later I learned a great deal more about negotiation while I was in the Ph.D. program and am now an ardent advocate of its use in humanitarian-aid projects as well as life in general.

Broadly viewed, negotiation is a conferring effort among two or more individuals or groups undertaken to reach an agreement—generally by exchanging promises and/or concessions. Equally broad are the three main contexts or realms from which negotiations take place: internationally, through public policy, and with individuals. The classification of two distinctive types of negotiation *Distributive* and *Integrative* are the heart of this discussion.

*Distributive negotiation* is what was described in the first paragraph above—very competitive and zero-sum gain—an effort filled taking a firm, unwavering stand on a particular issue. In other words, the proverbial example in the size of the pie is a fixed value, so if one party gains something, it is at the expense or loss of the other party. The negotiating partners may take on adversarial roles to achieve the highest individual gain.

*Integrative negotiation* is quite different and is accomplished when the parties cooperate with one another as partners in order to maximize benefits through the combining of interests into an agreement. The parties are negotiating with a desire to integrate the other party's needs, interests, aspirations, and preferences with their own in an agreement.

Integrative negotiation is achieved through information sharing and bargaining as well as a collective search for options, alternatives, and solutions. With integrative negotiation, the size of the pie is not a fixed value; it can be expanded in a manner whereby everyone can be a winner. No matter if it is a distributive negotiation or an integrative it can elicit emotion-clad responses from both parties.

## CROSS-CULTURAL NEGOTIATION

Emotions play an important part in the negotiation process. Emotions have the potential to play either a positive or negative role. During negotiations, the decision as to whether or not to settle rests in part on emotional factors. Negative emotions can cause intense and even irrational behavior, and can cause conflicts to escalate further causing negotiations to break down, but may be instrumental in attaining concessions. On the other hand, **Emotions play an** positive emotions often facilitate **important part in the** reaching an agreement and help **negotiation process.** to maximize joint gains, but can also be instrumental in attaining concessions. Humanitarian-aid projects are often brimming with emotion from all parties, as they usually include parties that are passionate about a particular cause. Positive and negative discrete emotions can be strategically displayed to influence task and relational outcomes and may play out differently across cultural boundaries. Keeping in mind that emotional responses are interpreted differently among cultures, various reactions can be expected, some will include behaviors that represent face-saving among the group, or may include total avoidance of any confrontation when in a group setting. These differences are not necessarily negative and can create huge potential benefits as well as huge problems if ignored. Cross-cultural negotiations are more complex than negotiations that take place in our own backyard, and may require Westerners to upgrade their listening skills, observational skills, and patience. But cross-cultural negotiations are also exciting, informative and an opportunity to gain local knowledge as we become better acquainted with our partners.

As you can well imagine, integrative negotiation is what I now use as a tool for achieving the greatest benefit from humanitarian-aid projects.

## INTEGRATIVE NEGOTIATION: GET READY, GET SET, GO

Even with integrative negotiation, where everyone is trying to look out for one another rather than maneuvering to take another's piece of the pie, it is appropriate and necessary that thorough preparation take place by all parties. Good preparation efforts permit reflection and focus on what each party will be bringing to the table, i.e., interests, objectives, resources, and constraints. Preparatory time also includes learning as much as possible about those who will be partnering at the negotiation table. Finally, and most importantly, preparatory efforts must include a systematic assessment of the situation to ensure that *every* stakeholder be properly identified and included in the negotiations. All too frequently, I have encountered negotiations that took place without representation of all the stakeholders. It does absolutely no good for donors and NGOs to negotiate the specifics of a humanitarian-aid project without the primary stakeholder—the beneficiary—being present, speaking, and being heard. Donors and NGOs may have the best of intentions, but without the presence of the beneficiary, the negotiations are incomplete and the stage is set for significant challenges and perhaps even project failure.

Looking back at the Indonesian educational sponsorship program and the interactions with Nyoman, I now realize we were engaging in the process of integrative negotiation, it was clumsy but that is what was happening. Nyoman was able to recognize that if he owned a water buffalo he would triple his production of rice, increase his income, and afford to send his children to school. The advantage to me? It would cost $250 to buy a water buffalo but it would decrease my fundraising efforts by $180 per year, taking me less than two years to break even on the investment. This turned into a win-win negotiation.

> ... ensure that every stakeholder be properly identified and included in the negotiations.

When all the stakeholders are identified and prepared, negotiations can proceed using a nine-step process. The steps assembled below both reflect and combine various elements found in most descriptions of steps for negotiation. However, the first step, which is extremely critical in multilingual, multicultural environments, is the critical need to establish a common domain for language. Following the systematic approach outlined below will increase the likelihood of a successful integrative-negotiation process:

### Nine-Step Process for Integrative Negotiation

1. Establish a common linguistic domain and a rapport (relationship building) among the negotiating parties.

2. Define the problem/issue(s) to be resolved, which is best accomplished through full disclosures, information sharing, and initial brainstorming with all major stakeholders.

3. Firmly establish the boundaries of the negotiation: the norms, the principles, and the rules to govern the negotiation process, i.e., how will anticipated impasses be resolved?

4. Determine how final decisions will be made. Discuss and adopt the rules and criteria for collective decision-making, whether through unanimity, consensus, majority voting, or whatever is the traditional practice of this community.

5. Identify and explore possible solutions, options, and alternatives, which can be accomplished through additional information sharing and brainstorming.

6. Identify the costs, benefits, and risks as well as the impacts or effects of each proposed alternative or solution. The identification process must include the short-term and long-term intended and unintended consequences of any actions taken.

7. Compare the alternatives in terms of collective costs, benefits, risks, and effects ratios and the previously agreed upon criteria for measuring success.

8. Select, adopt, and enact the alternative(s) or solution(s) using the decision-making method that was agreed upon earlier (see step 4).

9. As may be appropriate, evaluate and re-evaluate the decisions made. While evaluations normally occur

following the implementation phase of projects, it may also be appropriate to conduct evaluations throughout the lifetime of the project.

## AT THE NEGOTIATION TABLE—ONE MORE TIME

During the integrative-negotiation process, when many issues or factors related to the overall effort will be discussed, there will be times when the process stumbles over a single issue. Rather than continuing to labor over it, the parties may agree to set that one issue aside temporarily, but all parties must also acknowledge that an agreement has not been reached and that negotiations are not complete until that issue is returned to the table and resolved.

Even with the best intentions and negotiated outcomes, there may be times when particular elements of the agreement must be renegotiated. This occurs when certain conditions change or expectations have not been met. An example of conditions changing is the cost of materials rising between the time when the idea of constructing housing was conceptualized and the time when actual work begins. The change results in fewer houses for the available funds committed to the project. Though the education-through-food project had a successful outcome, the project manager in Guatemala considered renegotiating the agreement because the project's expectation of perfect attendance by the children was not being met. If renegotiation had occurred, the issue of the children attending school every day was not negotiable, but the project manager may have upped the groceries from one bag to two per family or perhaps offered transportation if that was preventing the children from attending every day.

Finally, never try to renegotiate when a project or

effort is "falling apart." If necessary, be willing to let the entire agreement fall apart and crumble. Under those dire circumstances, the negotiated agreement is closed and everything goes back on the table for consideration and fresh negotiation. The original process does not need to be considered a failure and a new negotiated process can build on the strengths of the prior effort. This kind of flexibility among the stakeholders is best accomplished when time has been taken to build a relationship.

## INTEGRATIVE NEGOTIATION—CREATING VALUE

Now that the disruptive what-ifs of negotiation have been presented, I'll return to the positive aspects of negotiation or, more specifically, integrative negotiation. While integrative negotiation is an indispensable process to examine and guide the achievement of intended goals or outcomes, it is also a means of creating value, because gains can be made by each of the parties involved. There is no reason to label the parties in terms of winners and losers when engaged in a win-win negotiation with the goal of cooperative effort in accomplishing a positive impact with a project. When the negotiations are complete and the process of moving forward with the desired goals and objectives is underway, it is critical that all parties stay true and consistent with the negotiated agreement through thick and thin, through trials and tribulations. By doing so, the parties uphold the tenets and particulars of the negotiated agreement, which were reached in a spirit of mutual support rather than in competition—really, it works!

*"A project is complete when it starts working for you, rather than you working for it."*

SCOTT ALLEN

---

CHAPTER TWELVE

# PROJECT MANAGEMENT— A ROAD MAP TO SUCCESS

Throughout this book, I've made repeated references to *projects*. Whether educating the children in the Indonesian village, obtaining medical supplies and equipment in Romania, or providing microloans in Nicaragua, all were referred to as projects. Each project experienced varying degrees of success, but their outcomes seemed to be more attributable to luck and perseverance than the lessons and principles outlined in this book. While I am forever grateful to have been a part of these projects, they were also my arena for learning, stumbling, and erring in pursuit of the best possible way to develop and complete sustainable humanitarian-aid projects. Had I known then what I share now, the road to project accomplishment would have been a great deal smoother, and I believe would have delivered a greater impact for all concerned.

A project can be broadly defined as a group or collective effort (*relationship building*) that is non-routine and undertaken to achieve one or more specific objectives (*negotiation outcomes*) using a variety of resources. The resources required (*with sustainability in mind*) can be any combination of time, space, energy, capital, human labor, communication systems, and, last but not least, creativity. How the project is undertaken is normally guided by a set of predefined methods and processes (*the project management path or cycle*). The following illustration depicts the expanded and refined version of the project-management cycle. See how the pieces or lessons are starting to come together—and coming together for a reason.

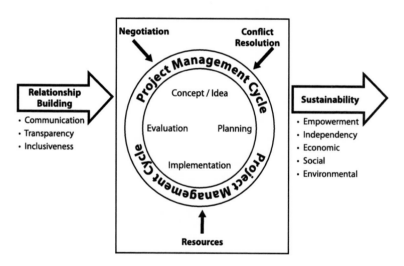

Just as other lessons shared, these are not confined to humanitarian aid, the lessons about projects are applicable to many aspects of our lives. Project management weaves the lessons together, bringing greater strength to the whole rather than relying on the single tensile strength of any one part, and it firmly guides the process to achieve the desired outcomes. Whether planning a self-improvement effort, a family vacation, or undertaking a community task, all are projects, and all would benefit from following a basic, defined path from start to finish.

## CHOOSING AN APPROACH

Projects almost always follow a path or life cycle that consists of four distinct but interrelated phases: concept/idea, planning, implementation, and evaluation. Each phase is critical in its own right and must be completed with the full knowledge and participation of the stakeholders. Shortcuts and incomplete efforts in any one phase are the start of a recipe for calamity. The following drawing presents two approaches to project management; the first is labeled Traditional Management Approach and the second is Inclusive Management Approach.

Basically top-down models are often characterized by a late or incomplete involvement of the primary beneficiaries at the start. The Inclusive Management approach is bottom-up and is more consistent with a grassroots' effort, making the primary beneficiaries a vital and integral component in idea and planning from the start. As with any depiction of a process, while the phases may appear linear and sequential, the reality is that the phases are dynamic and fluid, overlapping, and may even be repeated. A prime example is the frequent need for evaluation in every phase of the project cycle rather than an overall project evaluation at the end of the project. Based on the most current evaluation, the implementation process may change, therefore flexibility must remain in the forefront of our thinking. Too often I have witnessed absolutely no consideration for project evaluation, many organizations either do not find it worthwhile or have not included it in their expense budget and find it an unnecessary administrative cost. But it is an essential step in determining the strengths and weaknesses of any project so that current and future projects can build on successes without repeating errors.

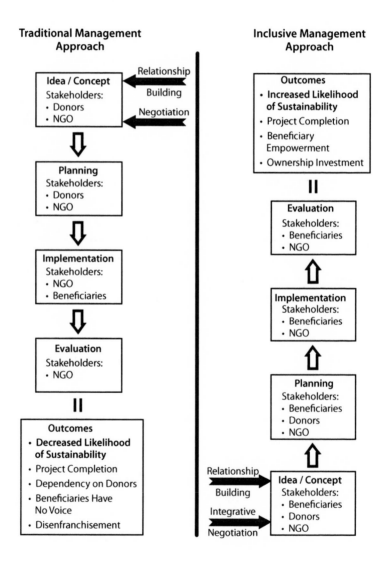

The first phase in project management is when *concepts* and *ideas* from the stakeholders begin to emerge. As depicted in the graph, relationship building and integrative negotiation are introduced at this point of the project-management effort. However, unless all of the stakeholders are present and their voices heard, the relationship building and integrative negotiation efforts can only be partial at best. In addition, vital local information, which may be known only by the beneficiaries, is missing when they have been excluded. All stakeholders must be represented and heard at the very first stage of the project-management cycle, during the stage of concept/idea. In humanitarian-aid projects, this initial phase includes identification of the problem/issue(s) to be resolved or the social needs to be addressed as well as the larger, targeted population of beneficiaries. This identification process can be accomplish using several different methods but my most successful method has included a system of Appreciative Inquiry, that builds on the assets already available to the community. During the concept/idea phase, objectives begin to emerge and a rough design of the solution to the problem/issue(s) or desired outcome is better and more realistically defined.

The second phase of project management is *planning*, and is widely regarded as the key to the successful completion of a project. Because of this, planning must also be viewed as a dynamic, continuous process that, even though thoroughly addressed in this phase, will be monitored and adjusted as necessary throughout the project's life cycle, regardless of its duration. Project planning duration is often described as short-term (one year), medium-term (three years), and long-term (five years). The planning phase incorporates an extensive list of project elements and precisely defines elements that were raised in the first phase as ideas, concepts, and the brainstorming session(s). Among the basics detailed in the planning phase are:

- Agreement on the specific objectives to be achieved through the project

- The resources that will be required to achieve these objectives, both internal and external

- Constraints of the project—economic, social, and environmental

- The specific processes and procedures that must/will be used to achieve the desired outcomes of the project

- The intended or expected benefits (in terms of outcomes, effects, and impacts as well as of outputs, results, or products)

- The complete set of costs and risks (economic, political, social-cultural, and environmental) associated with the attempt to generate the identified benefits

- The set of specific activities that will be carried out in order to minimize the costs and maximize the benefits, and who will carry out these responsibilities

- The timelines and schedules for such activities

Just as in the first phase, it is essential that all stakeholders be involved in the details and decisions and actions formulated in the planning stage. With such involvement, the stage will be properly set for proper project implementation.

Imagine in the bread-baking project in Romania if the girls that would be implementing the project had been involved in the idea/concept, planning, and implementation process. They most likely had the local knowledge that the oven would be located in an area where vandalism had occurred in the past and they could have informed us from the beginning we would need a security fence and it could have been included in our budget. The project manager, Sophia, was not from that geographic area. The girls also could have told us that our plan did not include much-needed bread-baking utensils and that they did not have the knowledge and skills to bake bread, or been trained in customer service, or how to market the product, nor were they financially literate. The age-old lesson "if it seems too good to be true, it probably is!" So expecting that a $500 oven would, by itself, turn into the vehicle that would pay for the educational expenses of dozens of girls, as it turned out, was too good to be true. Rather than slowing down and stepping through that meaningful process of including the beneficiaries as stakeholders and benefiting from local knowledge, Sophia forged ahead with my blessing, to begin the "sustainable project."

*Implementation* includes a timeline and process in which a project is actually executed in the field. For humanitarian projects, this also includes the acquisition of required supplies and equipment, their transformation through adequate processing, the delivery of the resulting infrastructure, products, or services to the targeted beneficiaries for their use, and the collection of information in order to evaluate and ultimately improve the performance of the project. Successful implementation rests largely with the project manager. The tasks of the project manager include directing and managing the project's resources and activities, continuous monitoring of progress to ensure the project remains on time and within budget, and directing corrective actions when necessary. All implementation actions are accomplished with the overall objective that the end product or service will meet the agreed specifications and standards for quality, which will ultimately be determined through evaluation of the project.

While the *evaluation* is generally depicted as the last

phase in a project-management cycle, it is clearly understood that evaluative efforts will be a continuous, pervasive process throughout the project. *Process evaluation*(s) focus on how the project is implemented (budgets, time schedules, process efficiencies, and synergy), while an *outcome evaluation* focuses on the nature and quality of the results or products of the project (effectiveness, equity, sustainability). As each step or phase of project management nears completion, evaluation of the efforts and outcomes within that phase may be a precursor or gateway to moving to the next phase. Stakeholders' agreement on the methods for evaluation determines the success of the project, who will be responsible for the evaluation, and when each evaluation will occur.

Project management provides the blueprint or map—from conception to final evaluation—and is a tool that integrates the other components of lessons learned. If we incorporate the essentials of relationship building and integrative negotiation keeping a watchful eye on project management, sustainability and resilience will produce programs that deliver a meaningful impact as a result of the efforts of all stakeholders.

*"Give a man a fish, he'll eat for a day. Give a woman microcredit, she, her husband, her children and her extended family will eat for a lifetime."*

BONO

Chapter Thirteen

# HOPE FOR A SUSTAINABLE FUTURE

As presented throughout this book, my decade plus of international humanitarian-aid efforts—whether visiting projects, working in the field, volunteering, promoting programs, or conducting research—provided invaluable opportunities and insight. I witnessed and evaluated numerous successful projects that either were well on the road or had the potential to become self-sustaining. There were also projects that failed; they did not deliver the intended impact and, in fact, caused harm. These projects, so heartbreaking in their failure to deliver sustainable outcomes, worse yet had created chronic, long-term dependency on donors. The originators of the projects failed to communicate the long-term strategy to achieve the outcome of sustainability and did not recognize the donors had only short-term intention for project support. During the educational sponsorship program in Indonesia I do not recall any donor asking the long-term strategy, or the anticipated length of the program, or if there was an exit plan in place. There are also projects that unintentionally create conflict within the community we are trying to "help."

Through these experiences, an in-depth understanding of certain principles has emerged. When given due consideration and applied as appropriate, these principles and lessons learned can assist in avoiding humanitarian-aid pitfalls as well as promote or support sustainable efforts. Perhaps the most important lesson of all was cementing in the understanding that above all else, preserving human dignity is the most important consideration of any project. I have come to understand that it is disrespectful to think or speak for others based on my preconceived notions of what they need and develop that into a successful project. This practice limits the opportunity for the beneficiaries to find their own voices and to speak for themselves. That has become a humbling reality for me in regard to humanitarian-aid projects because it is a lesson I learned long ago as a clinical psychologist, but neglected to apply to the field of humanitarian aid.

> It is disrespectful to think or speak for others based on my preconceived notions of what they need ...

## THE PEOPLE—DO NO HARM

As a solemn oath sworn before my peers, and one that has been at the heart of my efforts as a clinical psychologist for more than twenty years, is the principle of *do no harm*. Key to doing no harm is the learned and trained ability to observe people, their interactions, and how they present themselves. I can read genuine pride, satisfaction, self-esteem, and a sense of dignity on people's faces, see it in their eyes as they make eye contact with me and others, and even watch it in their stride and gait by the way they carry themselves. On the other side of the coin, I recognize shame, guilt, despair, low self-esteem, and lack of dignity as manifested through a reluctance to speak, downcast eyes, slumped shoulders, as well as a lack of sparkle in their eyes reflective of personal hope and dreams. While naively expecting only the former emotions to be present in the field as a result of humanitarian-aid efforts, I also observed the latter emotions more often than not and over time began to question why. In the beginning of my experience in the field, when I was holding physically starving babies and surrounded by malnourished toddlers as their mothers looked to me with hopeful eyes, it seemed anything that could be done to help would be better than doing nothing at all. The thought that my well-intended help might actually cause harm was the furthest thing from my mind.

So it seemed that if we just followed our hearts, even without an overall strategy with the goal of them accomplishing self-determination or even by using a poorly conceived approach to help all would eventually turn out for the best. After all, following our hearts was a known and well-worn path for helping others and there were always success stories to be told. It is difficult to be mindful of the appropriate financial strategy, cognizant of long-term planning requirements, or to keep the concept of a return on investment (ROI) at the forefront. Under the tried-and-true system, compassion acceptably trumped standard, best practices accounting systems, and efficient methodology.

Whenever I was involved in a project and being led by my heart, with an ability to influence others to donate their time, talent, and money the feelings were empowering, and I was part of something important and positive taking place in the world. It was a wonderful feeling! But when seeing or learning of failed projects, I often felt sad and discouraged; wondering why the beneficiaries had not kept the program progressing forward or at least maintained a status quo. There was a faulty and erroneous assumption on my part that the fruits of our time, talent, and resources would continue long after we had left, because it was important to the people we were trying to "help." It took looking beyond the short-term benefits and toward the long-term goal of sustainability and reliance before the answers became clear.

*Now* it seems so simple to understand why the beneficiaries did not, could not, maintain the program(s). They did not have the same access as I did to resources (the donors), to capture and maintain their interest to keep the financial resources flowing. In reality, we—the good, intentioned donors from afar—contributed to building dependency rather than to programs that were self-sustaining by the people. If a program is creating dependency rather than self-sufficiency, it is a violation of the do no harm tenet. Even though it was unintended, the impact carried the consequence of causing harm.

## OUT WITH THE OLD, IN WITH THE NEW

The old systems approach to humanitarian aid was fairly simple, or so it seemed. Most of us can pretty easily identify our personal interest when in the field, whether in education, health, agriculture, soil, or environmental and that is the area we may be drawn to when we see others do not have the perceived need met. It is not too difficult to select a cause. Our hearts, experience, and knowledge pull us in certain directions when visiting a developing country. With our well-nourished, formally educated brain we can efficiently identify the problems, education for children, housing for the homeless living at the city dump, clean water for those drinking from contaminated rivers and streams, access to health care and education for those lacking in knowledge, effective agricultural practices—all necessities and priorities depending on our personal Western perspective. We return home, tell the stories of others in need, pull at the heartstrings of others, show our pictures of people in need, and begin raising funds to meet the perceived needs of the beneficiaries. An even simpler approach is to listen to the stories that have traveled to the field and donate from the comfort of our home. We have all seen the television commercials asking for monetary support to feed starving children or educate them, and for years most of us have stepped up to the cause on

> ... the conditions of our "help," at times, may have violated cultural traditions ...

many different levels and have shared our resources with the intention of "helping."

Unfortunately, the conditions of our "help," at times, may have violated cultural traditions or provided resources/ equipment that the beneficiaries have no way of using or maintaining. Even a more basic flaw was that the beneficiaries and the donors may not have agreed on what the problem or need was or the solution, but the donors still made their own judgment of the situation and rendered a solution, without adequately consulting the beneficiaries. I visited one project where an NGO in the field had asked for the donation of used hospital beds because all medical patients were lying on the floor, making it difficult to treat them and leaving them vulnerable to even more infections. As I approached the medical building I saw what seemed to be hundreds of beds, not in the medical building, but outside, exposed to the elements, rusted and now of no use. When I questioned the program manager about the rusted equipment, he told me they had sent out a request for used hospital beds, he neglected to mention in his request that the medical building had no electrical power. The generous donors from the U.S. medical center sent used electrically powered beds that were sent in an upright position and were of no value to this center. The field medical center needed the old-fashioned, hand-crank beds. We need to always remember the cardinal rule of asking the right questions and then listening to the answers.

## NEED FOR RESOURCES

If only money was needed to fix the problem of poverty, it would have, or should have been fixed a long time ago. Respected economist Jeffery Sacks, formally from the World Bank and the United Nations, tells us the gap between the rich and poor is getting wider and deeper. If so, where are the benefits of our generous charitable giving of money going? In the U.S. alone, billions of dollars are being generated and disbursed annually by service clubs, church groups, civic groups, individual humanitarians, and nonprofit organizations to name a few. And yet, the United Nations reports more than 40 percent of the human population is living on less that $2 per day, resulting in 24,000 preventable deaths daily! What is happening with the resources that are being shared? We know there are humanitarian-aid systems designed to "help." But when these systems are developed, implemented, and evaluated only through the lens of the donor, the likelihood of creating a sustainable impact is greatly diminished. A significant change in our approach to helping others is needed. We need a shift in the paradigm, one that more closely relates the problem to the solution. Incorporating the beneficiary as a primary stakeholder, and local knowledge, are integral components in the needed change. Some of the promising grassroots' methods that are leading toward closing the gap between the rich and the poor has been through the acknowledgment of local knowledge, identifying all major stakeholders, and allowing each to express their voice and choices, relationship building, and utilizing the tools of integrative negotiation.

## DEVELOPING THE NEW APPROACH

The new approach to sustainable humanitarian aid begins at the bottom rather than the top. Building from the ground up or as a grassroots effort incorporates the deliberate actions of involving the beneficiary stakeholder throughout all phases of project planning. It also begins with a series of questions rather than assumptions. *We must stop assuming that we know the answers to other people's problems and start asking the most basic questions.* Following is a sampling or flavor of this bottom-up, grassroots, and inclusive approach.

- Would your community benefit from additional resources?

- If so, what resources would have the greatest impact on the most people?

- Do you think there is a problem? If you do, what is the problem?

- What assets and skills are already available to remedy this situation?

- What has already been accomplished in an effort to remedy this situation?

- What progress has been made?

- What has worked? What has not worked?

- What resources do you have available?

- Do you want to partner in searching for solutions?

- In what ways can we work together to build on what has or can work, using available resources?

An even better initiation to the new, inclusive, open communication regarding a potential project is permitting the potential beneficiaries to approach the NGO, service club, church group, or humanitarian in the field to offer their identification of the problem and ideas toward solutions.

## MICROFINANCE SYSTEMS EMERGE

*"Microfinance is an idea whose time has come."*
KOFI ANNAN, UN SECRETARY-GENERAL

Microcredit is the extension of very small loans (microloans/credit) designed to encourage entrepreneurship among people lost in the never-ending generational cycle of poverty.

These individuals lack collateral, steady employment, and a verifiable credit history and are systematically denied the opportunity to define their own path to escape the grip of poverty. As such, they cannot meet even the most minimal qualifications to gain access to traditional credit. These individuals are systematically denied traditional resources for borrowing money, and are desperate to rise out of poverty, they are, indeed, society's most economically and socially vulnerable. Unfortunately, they often fall prey to loan sharks and other avenues that drive them deeper into the pit of despair, hopelessness, and an endless cycle of economic poverty.

Dr. Muhammad Yunus has developed arguably the best known and most respected microfinance model in the world through the Grameen Bank in Bangladesh. The model is based on the idea that regardless of being poor, the intended beneficiaries have skills that are underutilized and often not recognized. Dr. Yunus and the Grameen Bank were awarded the Nobel Peace Prize in 2006 for his "effort to create economic and social development from below."

Numerous research studies have reported the benefits and advantages of microfinance systems being at the core of developing microenterprises. Similarly, throughout my years of project-evaluation efforts, the programs that gave me the most hope included adequate resources. The greatest positive for the beneficiaries were programs that allowed them the opportunity to develop their own solutions to living in poverty. Microfinance systems microloans, microcredit, micro savings, and micro insurance for their entrepreneurial endeavors have the potential to follow this pattern of success. And in doing so, increase the likelihood of creating sustainable projects, thereby furthering resilient community development, leading to prosperity, and contributing significantly to ending poverty.

## Group Lending Model

The Group Lending Model is a method of disbursing microloans to borrowers. The individual borrowers are members of a group that meets weekly at a borrower's home or community center for the payment on a loan and they receive practical education regarding general literacy, along with financial literacy skills, and general health information. Rather than financial lending being based on traditional collateral, this culture encourages financial responsibility where peer support leads to a 99 percent rate of repayment of loads to include interest. Monetary loans are made to small groups or cooperatives, and the group approves the loans by determining who is a reliable borrower. Peer pressure, derived through geographic and social ties, is used as a means of ensuring loan payment. Group members benefit from mutual support and shared accountability. In addition, group-based lending is more efficient and lowers the transaction costs for the provider of the loans.

This model is often used within microfinance systems and has produced many benefits that exceed that of making money available to the poor. Independently, the model has been used to develop lending circles, increase the community's social capital, and provide training related to personal health, literacy, best-business practices, and requisite financial skills. Through this exposure to training, group members are more likely to value education and send their children to school. Collectively, the benefits of the Group Lending Model increases the likelihood of successful individual enterprises as well as business expansion brought about through networking with group members. In addition, the success of the Group Lending Model and the individuals within the groups potentially generates more disposable income, which can lead to community-wide project planning and enhancements.

> ... group members are more likely to value education and send their children to school.

Finally, and most importantly, the outcomes of the Group Lending Model are pride, dignity, empowerment, choice, self-determination, voice, and sustainability.

## SOCIAL BUSINESS

The concept of social business, as first defined by Professor Muhammad Yunus, is a natural extension of microfinance, in that it includes the capacity to develop an organization or company intended to address a social need. The objective of the organization is to achieve social goal(s), such as education, health, environmental, or as identified by a specific community, done so in a manner that meets the expectation of sustainability.

Traditionally, there are two distinct methods of conducting business: *for-profit* companies that utilize best-business practices intended to maximize profits and pay dividends to private investors. The other primary business model, the *nonprofit* organization, does not accumulate financial resources, most often focuses on a social need and frequently is dependent on individual donors, governments, and foundation grants to meet their annual budgets and does not pay dividends to donors. Many social needs are often met by nonprofit organizations that range from food banks to sponsoring the arts and cultural community programs.

Social business differs from even the nonprofit business model. While it may be initially funded philanthropically, a social business is expected to generate a modest profit, have the ability to repay the initial investors if they so desire, and address a social objective. The profit from a social business will also be used to expand the organization's reach, as well as improve the product or service in other ways to subsidize the social mission. The success of a social business is measured by the positive impact on the people, the environment, or a social cause rather than the amount of profit produced over a given period of time.

In his book *Creating a World without Poverty–Social Business and the Future of Capitalism*, Dr. Yunus defines two types of social business. The first (Type I) focuses on providing a product and/or service that identifies a specific social, ethical, or environmental goal. A prominent example is Grameen Danone. The second (Type II) is a profit-oriented business owned by the poor or other underprivileged members of a society who can gain by receiving direct dividends or indirect benefits. An example of this type is the Grameen Bank located in Bangladesh, founded by Dr. Yunus and now owned by the poor people it was designed to help. The organization and Dr. Yunus were awarded the Nobel Peace Prize in 2006 for its impact on the poor at a grassroots level.

## APPRECIATIVE INQUIRY

The systems of microfinance, including social business and all efforts leading to sustainability, have the ability to fully incorporate the principles of Appreciative Inquiry (AI) as a tool used in assessment. Appreciative Inquiry is an *asset-based approach* based on the concept of recognizing the most favorable conditions and assets of a community or culture and fostering positive, empowering relationships. It asks basic questions: What is already working well? What is good? What are the strengths of the current situation? Stakeholders are motivated to understand value, recognize the most-favorable conditions of the current culture, and foster positive, empowering relationships. The opposite approach to AI, and one that is frequently used in organizations, focuses on what is wrong, which suggests ineffectiveness or inefficiency and fosters the practice of "blame."

The concept of AI is rooted in *positive psychology*. The idea for its success is to build on strengths rather than making faults and weaknesses the primary focus. In doing so, stakeholders are motivated to go forward with appreciation and build on strengths, to move from one success or achievement to another, and ultimately get better as they progress to exceptional performance.

## RECOGNIZING SUCCESSFUL PROJECTS

Successful and sustainable community economic-development projects have been studied at length and found to possess certain strategic commonalities. By far, the systems that lead toward sustainability have most consistently incorporated the following seven factors in the area of microfinance.

To help frame successful projects, these factors are shared:

1. Successful projects gave voice and listened to the intended beneficiary. The byproduct of this factor was empowerment, dignity, respect, and choice.

2. They provided an opportunity for the beneficiaries to resolve their own issues of poverty and develop a sustainable model that was unique to their environment and culture.

3. NGOs, project managers, and donors considered the beneficiaries as major stakeholders and included them in a primary stakeholder role in all four stages of project management: ideas/concept, planning, implementation, and evaluation.

4. The continuance of the project was not dependent on attracting the goodwill of long-term donors.

5. The successful projects had an ongoing evaluation process present at each stage of the project-management cycle.

6. Each project had an exit strategy from external influences (i.e., provision of resources).

7. Successful projects were driven by the request of potential beneficiaries rather than imposed on communities by well-intentioned donors who identified the needs of the communities as viewed through the lens of outsiders.

## IT'S A SUSTAINABLE WRAP

Over the years, while working in the area of economic community development, I have come to believe that charity robs people of their voice, choice, and dignity as well as having the potential to entrap both donors and beneficiaries in a never-ending cycle of dependency. In stark contrast to charity, systems of microfinance—to encompass microloans, social business, and appreciative inquiry—result in people acting with pride, dignity, voice, choice, and self-confidence. They have been afforded the opportunity of self-determination through entrepreneurship, insuring the success of sustainability, resilience, and prosperity to create their own solutions to poverty. More recent experiences in the field and supporting research inspire me to believe that the world of humanitarian aid is moving in the right direction. Microfinance provides a new paradigm for helping others without creating or causing harm. Rather, it encourages self-determination through self-sufficiency. Proper implementation of microfinance models has the ability to change the world, ultimately leading to people living in peace through the alleviation of poverty. The existing models offer an exciting vision and pathway toward greater opportunity for all humans regardless of their country of birth. It is a future that relies not solely on hope and charity or a temporary handout, but rather on effective methodologies that lend people a hand UP, driving humanitarian aid in a more powerful, impactful direction. Every effort, no matter the size, born of respect for all mankind and mindful of human dignity for all will surely contribute to a better world.

The words of cultural anthropologist Margaret Mead have served as an inspiration to many others and me:

*"Never doubt that a small group of thoughtful, committed citizens can change the world. Indeed, it is the only thing that ever has."*

MARGARET MEAD

# EPILOGUE

This book began with reference to a single strand of life's journey and the twists and turns often necessary to arrive at one's final destination. Each of us has our own journeys; this is part of my life journey. It includes lessons of pride and humility, heartbreak and empathy, curiosity and fulfillment. Within me is a personal sense of responsibility to share resources that we often take for granted; I agree with these timeless words of wisdom: "to those that much is given, much is expected." I am ever cognizant and grateful for the opportunities available to those of us fortunate enough to be born in a developed country.

My journey is far from over; the process of learning is both fluid and dynamic in my life. What I share in this book is but a pause along the journey's way; an opportunity for me to gather some of the lessons learned. Lessons shared have a much broader application than from where they were derived. They are not limited to the field of humanitarian aid, but may be adopted or adapted by businesses, institutions, schools, and individuals seeking the best possible outcomes to any of life's situations. What I share is not with the sense that I have arrived with all the answers, but rather, shared in the sense that this is what I know at this time. After searching, stumbling, observing, and researching, I share what I believe to be vital components in resolving issues and challenges confronting all citizens of the world. My experiences would not have been possible without the willingness of others to share their journeys with me.

The lessons were assembled over the years and began with Nyoman's simple but penetrating question, "Did I really want to help?" His question led me to start digging deeper, going beyond the all-too-common thinking and approaches to humanitarian aid. With each project I became involved in, there were lessons to be learned. Just about the time I thought I was on the right course, there was another straightforward question posed to me—this time by a professor. He asked, "Do you think that humanitarian aid could or ever causes conflict?" This was a question that most probably I would never have asked myself. My mind would not have let me imagine that our projects ever had the potential of causing conflict. His question and my subsequent investigation into such a possibility took me from working in the field with humanitarian projects to back in the classroom. During this period of academics, additional lessons were drawn from textbooks as well as through discussions with international colleagues. The advantage and culmination of the academic experience was the opportunity to return to the field to complete research as an unbiased observer. The research produced valuable findings and lessons. Collectively, these are my lessons learned through personal discovery, which was often guided by the patience, understanding, and goodwill of others, at times while they shared their lessons with me.

Best wishes and blessings in walking your own path of discovery, finding your own water buffalos, and attending to the difficult questions asked by others that help us grow. May the rewards and lessons learned be abundant and bring positive change to you, your family, your community, and the world. With each successful discovery or project completed, there will always be more learning on the horizon. May we all benefit from the sharing of our life's lessons to build a more equitable world, so that we all may live with dignity and opportunity.

*"The future depends on what we do in the present. Be the change you wish to see in the world."*

MAHATMA GANDHI

# APPENDIX: RESEARCH PROJECTS

## Economic Community Development through Housing Project

### Housing and Micro Farms

*Project Objective:*

To develop a new sustainable community for the families currently living in extreme poverty at or near a city dump in Central America.

*Project Description:*

The new community would provide a home, clean water, sanitation facilities, electricity, nutritional supplements, education costs for the children, medical, and health services, and the essential components including plantings to develop a micro farm. The project goals reflected the intention that each family within the development community be self-sustaining within a two-year period of time, given a donor contribution of $2,500 per family.

*Non-Governmental Organizations (NGOs):*

Eight NGOs formed a partnership to complete this project. The partnership purchased land approximately six miles from the city dump, with enough property to provide forty-three homes. The partnership agreed that one NGO would serve as the primary contractor for the community development and a project manager would be hired to oversee the entire project on behalf of all eight NGOs. Each partner NGO was assigned responsibility for different phases of project management (design/concept, planning, implementation, and evaluation).

*Beneficiaries:*

The potential beneficiaries were informed about the project through announcements made at the city dump regarding informational meetings that would be held to inform the interested parties of the criteria necessary to qualify for a home in the new community. The beneficiaries were to notify the municipal social workers if they were interested in attending the meeting; they were then given times, dates, and transportation to the location of the meeting, if needed. Approximately 300 families were initially interested in attending the first informational meeting; this group was split into smaller groups that were more manageable for communication with the local and NGO social workers. Following the informational meeting, if a family was still interested in the housing community, the next step was for the families to agree to an interview with the municipal social worker. The interviews included the entire family group, as well as individual family members; again the families were provided transportation to the interview site.

Future residents were told during the interview process that each family would be expected to invest labor/sweat-equity hours in the building of the homes and this would be their contribution to the purchase of the home. They were informed that each family would work their own micro farm, use the produce for family consumption, and surplus product could be sold at the market for additional income. Other general rules shared at the time of the interviews included that children were expected to attend school, and fees would be paid for the first two years by the NGO until the family had the ways and means to pay their school fees by growing additional crops; there would be zero tolerance for domestic abuse or any violence, and/or the abuse of drugs or alcohol. The residents of the community were expected to behave as a "community" by acting as good neighbors and responding to one another with courtesy and respect. They would be expected to collaborate on decisions for the good of the community and resolve their own conflicts.

*Donors:*

In the philanthropic world, individual donors, foundations, and NGOs were invited to become financial partners with the understanding that by donating $2,500 per family, the individual families and the community would be self-sustaining within two years.

*Project Analysis:*

During the onsite interview, the project manager was asked if she believed this was an example of a successful/sustainable economic community development project; the manager stated the following,

> "We have not accomplished what we set out to do, and we have unknowingly and unwillingly built a dependency for the beneficiaries on this Foundation."

When asked if the beneficiaries were part of negotiations in order to contribute ideas about how to solve the problems of being homeless and living on the edge of the city dump, reach agreements regarding project objectives, societal goals and cultural values, or define successful project outcomes. The project manager further stated,

> "We do not, nor will we negotiate with the beneficiaries regarding project objectives, the planning, or the budget concerning the community development projects, or the intended outcome of the project; all of this is decided with the donors before we even hit the ground at the project site."

In other words, the identification of the problem, the solutions to the problem, indeed the project itself was determined by the staff of an NGO or an outside volunteer associated with a nonprofit organization.

They did negotiate with the beneficiaries concerning their willingness to perform sweat-equity hours for ownership of a house, but the number of hours required is already predetermined prior to input from the beneficiaries. The beneficiaries are able to help determine who in the family will actually perform the work, and if the work performance can include an extended family member.

One of the strengths of the project is that funding is stable and it appears that it will be ongoing for an undesignated length of time. The partner NGO has access to numerous shared resources, both financial and human capital, through a steady stream of volunteers. The physical relocation of forty-three impoverished families living at the dump has been accomplished. The families now have access to safe water but only through the services of a delivery truck visiting the community one time per week. Latrines were provided but no electricity has been provided nor has the drilling for a water well occurred as of yet because the project has grossly exceeded the budget as planned. The initial donors were told it would be a two-year project, and at the time of this research evaluation, the project was well into the seventh year of dependency on the NGOs for funding, as was the Western-born project manager dependent on donors for a salaried position.

Consistent with many community development projects, the majority of the negotiations take place between the NGOs and the donors of the project, in that the beneficiaries were not considered stakeholders in the project until the implementation stage of the project cycle; all conceptual ideas, planning and budgetary guidelines for the project occur prior to involving the local population.

There is a considerable disadvantage to the geographic location of this community development project. This housing project is located six miles from the site of the city dump where the beneficiaries had been living, so the residents of the project continue to walk back to the dump daily to collect the scraps of metal, wire, glass, and paper to sell to recyclers to acquire currency. This is a necessary daily trek because the beneficiaries still do not have their microfarms that were intended to give them economic stability through the sale of their surplus produce at the market. Some of the residents continue to stay at the dump site for several days and then return to the housing project for a few days. Another weakness of the location is that the homes were built four miles from the nearest school and the children require transportation. This is an additional community expense: a bus, a driver, insurance, and fuel that was not in the original budget and will be difficult for the residents to maintain without the assistance of the NGO.

Onsite interviews with the beneficiaries confirmed the responses of the project manager—that they were not included: (a) in the process of problem identification, (b) in potential solutions, (c) in the budget, or (d) in the planning of the project. When there was finally a possibility to negotiate specific areas with beneficiaries as stakeholders, the negotiation occurred with major limitations. The NGOs had already negotiated with multiple partners regarding most of the parameters of the project, constraining their ability to remain flexible when negotiating with beneficiaries. A beneficiary stated in an interview,

> *"We are never asked what we want, we are told what we will get and then told to solve the problem ourselves, if it is not enough or not what we wanted."*

The project plan did not consider the short- or long-term environmental impact of the housing units and the activities of residents in the area. Trees and plant life were destroyed to build the housing community and still have not been replaced and there is not a plan to replenish the environment. The current residents have cut down the remaining trees for firewood and, unless reforestation occurs, the next generation will be affected by the lack of vegetation in the community.

The original plan for each family to have a micro farm did not occur. There was an unanticipated issue with the water supply that prohibits the planting of individual gardens. The project managers had negotiated funds for a specific number of housing units, as the price of materials increased; the money that had been budgeted for the water well was directed toward housing construction. Currently fresh water is brought into the village on a weekly basis by truck. The residences do share a very small community garden, but it appears neglected and adequate crops cannot be harvested to supply all the families or to sell surplus at the market. The failed micro farm aspect of the community plan has had a serious impact on the families and compromises their ability to secure fresh food.

The residents on this project have become dependent on the NGOs as a source of shelter and food. The residents have been neither empowered nor trained to make effective collective decisions regarding project operations, and they have difficulty making individual decisions in the project community since, in the past, they have always made decisions based on self-interest. They must now understand how their individual decisions affect others in the community. There has been little interest or investment on the part of the partner NGOs to provide training in capacity building for the beneficiaries so at some point they can manage their own community. At this time, the residents remain financially, socially, and culturally dependent on external factors to determine the parameters in their lives.

## Housing Sweat Equity for Sustainability

### Less than $1 per week

*Project Objective:*
To build a community that would become self-sustaining within a two-year period of time.

*Project Description:*
This is a relocation project for families living in extreme poverty at or near a local city dump; this project is located in a different country than the first project. These families are dependent on the products of the dump for food and recyclables that they gather and sell to vendors. Their average income is approximately one dollar per week per family, and they have no access to fresh food, nearby potable water, electricity, or health services. The children appear malnourished and dehydrated with thinning hair, including a reddish tint at the ends, missing teeth, and many with distended bellies. They do not attend school because they must help their families

at a very early age to search in the dump for food and gather recyclables to sell for cash.

The property was donated to the NGO and it was intended to include a small two-room school, a communal garden to partially supplement the family's nutritional needs, with the surplus sold at the market producing a profit designated for community improvements and the sustainability of the community. This project would also include the provision of water for personal use and agricultural needs, electricity, and sanitation with latrines.

*NGO:*

This project was begun and maintained by a single well-funded NGO in the United States; they have been involved in charity work in Central America for the past 20+ years. This NGO attracts donor funding and thousands of volunteer hours per year.

*Beneficiaries:*

The potential beneficiaries were informed about the pending project by social workers from one of the four NGOs that partnered to fund and manage the project. The social workers made daily visits to the dump area and began informal conversations, targeting women with small children as the desired potential residents. Time was scheduled for informational meetings, word traveled through the population by word of mouth, and signs were posted at the site of the dump. At the first meeting, more than 400 families showed interest in learning information regarding the new community housing.

The selection process began with families that had young children living with them at the site of the dump. The family interviews were highly structured and initially held with groups of ten to twelve people, with social workers from the NGOs intending to observe the interaction of the people with one another. The NGO staff stated they were observing to determine if the families interacted with one another, or if they isolated themselves, and if there appeared to be actions that signaled cooperation, and if leadership within the group naturally occurred. The staff used this information in the selection process for the new residents.

More interviews were later conducted with smaller and smaller groups until finally individual families were interviewed. The staff had constructed semi-structured interviews and scored the responses from potential residents with the intention of matching certain individuals to create what they thought would eventually become a good blend of personalities in the community. They also used this information to assign people to the housing units and attempted to identify which families would make good neighbors.

The project social worker shared with the researcher that this did not result in an effective method of screening people; as the interviews took place, the questions were shared by the residents and they began to give very similar responses, which they thought were the "right answers"—what the interviewers/social workers wanted to hear. Some potential residents were deceptive in their responses regarding issues like domestic violence. When the project staff did not recognize the deception or similar pattern of reply, the staff made erroneous assumptions about the new residents and acted accordingly.

For instance, the mother of the family may not have been honest about the existence of domestic violence within the family so that she could hopefully secure a home for herself and the children. Then, after moving into the residence, behaviors such as alcoholism and domestic abuse began to emerge and the community and staff were unprepared for the resulting problems. The residents did not have effective problem-solving skills and continued to defer to the project staff to resolve domestic problems. The staff is in the process of rectifying the problem by providing training in assertiveness skills to the individual families.

The potential residents were told that they were expected to invest sweat-equity hours to gain ownership of their new house. They would also be assisted by onsite volunteers sponsored by the NGO to physically build a community. A small school would also be built on the site to provide education for the children. Children would be required to attend school daily rather than make the daily trip to the dump with the parents. There was also adequate space for small animals, such as chickens, rabbits, and goats. The potential residents were told that they would engage in collective decision making and help decide what would be preferred community projects and perhaps individually or collectively raise and care for the livestock.

Following the interview process, thirty families were selected to become the initial residents of the new community project.

*Donors:*

Individuals and organizations that had historically donated to this NGO were asked to support one family by donating $3,200. The NGO was convinced that the families in the project would be economically self-sustaining within a two-year period of time.

*Project Analysis:*

The NGOs used donated land approximately two miles from the city dump, with enough property to provide fifty homes with a communal micro farm. The NGO hired a Western-born project manager to oversee the entire project.

The NGOs and residents have successfully built twenty-seven of the intended fifty homes. The funding from the NGOs is limited but it does appear stable according to the project manager. Due to less funding than anticipated and more expenses than the budget planned for, there is no preparation underway to build the remaining twenty-three homes. Limited electricity during specific hours of the day has been provided for the community, and the water is currently being trucked to the community weekly because the water-well digging effort was unsuccessful. The goal of individual home latrine sanitation has not been accomplished and there is not a plan currently in place to accomplish the task.

Many trees and vegetation were cleared for construction and there is not a plan in place for reforestation. The sustainability of the ecosystem is threatened due to lack of latrines and trees and vegetation; this will have a progressively negative impact on current residents and future generations if it remains unaddressed.

When the project manager was interviewed onsite and

questioned about whether this project is considered successful and sustainable, the manager frankly responded,

> "No, we have not done what we set out to do. We should have taught these people to fish, but instead we keep bringing boatloads of fish to them."

There seemed to be frustration in the voice of the project manager as he responded. When asked if the NGOs had negotiated with the beneficiaries concerning the identification of the problem of living in extreme poverty on the city dump, or to determine the priorities of the families, or to find solutions and alternatives to the stated problem, or the project objectives, societal values, or program evaluation, the manager responded no. He further stated,

> "We can't negotiate with the beneficiaries at the beginning of the project cycle because we don't even know who specifically will be the people accepted into the project. These people don't know how to negotiate, or what is best for them, or what the possibilities might be, they have never lived in a community like this, we need to teach them how to do all of that."

The beneficiaries' voices mirrored the responses of the project manager; they stated that they were not included in the decision-making process for any components of the project.

> "They have asked us nothing, we just hear how it is supposed to be and if we do not do it, they tell us we can leave. Yes, leave after we have helped them build their houses they keep calling them ours, but I don't think so."

The residents also seemed confused and frustrated that the promised resources were not delivered and they clearly stated general mistrust of the NGO and the project manager. The residents expressed a concern that had not been heard before, that they felt

> "... unsafe in the community because gangs of unhappy young people were forming, they steal from everyone and threaten us all with safety."

Later the project manager confirmed that there had been vandalism and theft in the community and the staff was in the process of developing a team of concerned citizens/residents to determine how to best respond to the situation. The project manager surmised that the former life that the youth had experienced living at the dump was more stimulating to them; they were more invisible and able to wander without interference—very different than life in this isolated, quiet, new community where most activity is transparent. The community is not in a position to be protected by the local police department due to its location and the difficult roads to get to the area. The residents have explained that notifying the police for protection, or any outside authority, does not occur in this culture for many reasons that will not be explained at this time.

There remain wonderful opportunities for the practice of integrative negotiation in this community if the beneficiaries are viewed as primary stakeholders and become part of the resolution determination process. The community remains dependent on the NGO for resources and economic support, even though they have far exceeded the intended two-year mark to become self-sustaining; at the time of this evaluative research, they have been in existence for five years. This community has a multitude of areas that are ripe for the residents to be involved in developing the resolution to problems. There appear to be two frustrated parties: the NGO/staff and the residents within the community. If they began with a community meeting to identify the problems, then establish the priorities and what will be addressed, and in what order, they will begin to create an atmosphere of collaboration rather than dependency. If the residents of the community were to identify leaders and were given the occasion to demonstrate leadership in a way that is congruent with their culture, the dependency on the NGO staff would begin to melt as empowerment of the beneficiaries grows.

This community project is not self-sustaining, and, under the current system of management, it is not likely that it will become sustainable. There is high probability that the community can become a place that represents the goals, societal values, dreams, and aspirations of the residents if the model of multi-cultural integrative negotiation is implemented properly.

# Landless Farm Families

*Project Objective:*

Build an economically sustainable community that is geographically safe.

*Project Description:*

This is a community housing project that is targeted for rural impoverished farm families that have been dislocated from their properties following an extended civil war that included the confiscation of their farmland. The farm population was provided some housing by the government and moved to the outskirts of a large city to live in precarious dwellings on the slopes of dangerous ravines. They are no longer property owners, as their parents and grandparents had been, and they are considered squatters on government land. Approximately 150,000 families live in conditions of extreme poverty, in makeshift housing on dirt floors that are often washed or blown down the ravines in high winds and during the rainy season. They have no sanitation (latrines), electricity, or access to clean water. They subsist on the food items they can collect at the city dump where they scavenge for materials such as paper, glass, copper wire, and metals that can be sold.

This humanitarian community development project was actually conceived years after damage caused by Hurricane Mitch. The declared objectives of the project were to: (1) build a sustainable community that is geographically safe, including a school and medical clinic; (2) provide access to clean water, power, and latrines; (3) provide opportunity for change in the lives of impoverished people; and (4) build a sustainable community that may serve as a model program that could be duplicated throughout the region.

*NGO:*

This project was begun and maintained by multiple NGOs based in the United States; they have provided humanitarian aid in Central America for the past decade. This particular group of NGOs has not partnered in the past. This project attracts donor funding and thousands of volunteer hours per year.

*Beneficiaries:*

The representative of the NGO stated that the beneficiaries were "self-selected" following information notifications displayed at various community gathering places, including churches. Several informational meetings were held, during which the attendees were given specifics about the project's objectives, as well as the eligibility rules and criteria developed by the NGO to qualify for a residence in the community.

After a selection process that consisted of several meetings and family interviews with social workers and staff from the NGO, seventy-five applicant families were found to meet all the eligibility criteria. The NGO staff reported that as more detailed rules and requirements were introduced, many families began to withdraw their applications, assuming they either did not meet the criteria or were unwilling to follow the pre-established rules. Following another long screening process, lasting six months, fifteen families were eventually selected to be the first community residents.

Immediately following the selection, the families were expected to take part in the construction of the houses by providing labor that would be considered sweat equity toward the ownership of their new home. To perform the sweat equity, transportation was needed to get the beneficiaries to and from the new community location site. Their work efforts were not necessarily directed to the home they would ultimately own, but rather to a group of homes, and individual home assignments would be determined at a later date. The actual building of the homes was intended to occur in the spirit of a team-building event among the residents and volunteers representing the NGO.

At the time of the research there were forty-two families living in the new community, which at that time was five years old, with the plan to increase the number of families by twenty in the next year, which would then include a total of sixty-two families. As the community continues to grow, the screening process has changed with each new group moving in; with lessons learned, the admission process remains fluid. This NGO did identify the goal of building a sustainable community but did not plan a timeline on when it would be completed.

*Project Analysis:*

During the onsite evaluation and interview, the project manager was asked "Do you consider this a successful/sustainable community development project?" The manager responded,

> *"We have failed miserably at community development, we have helped some families, but our objective was to build a healthy community where residents could sustain themselves and future generations; we have only built houses."*

When asked if the NGO had negotiated with the beneficiaries of the project concerning problem identification, possible solutions, societal values, project objectives, and evaluation of outcomes, the response was no. The first area of negotiation with beneficiaries occurred in the project-implementation stage when the future residents were told about the sweat-equity hours needed to qualify for a house in the new community. The number of hours was predetermined by the NGO and not negotiable, but how the hours would be performed was negotiated. For instance, if a future resident did not have good building skills or if there were enough builders for the day, a resident could earn sweat-equity hours by cleaning the administration building instead of building.

A high-ranking officer in this NGO stated during the onsite interview that this organization defines *sustainability* as a "project having the ability to gain the attention and interest of donors, and to attract funds from donors on a long-term basis." He further stated that "having their entire budget dependent on donors was, in fact, sustainable because they have a diverse base of donors and, from a historical perspective, this NGO has survived and grown for the past twenty years." He shared his belief that "having a diversified and consistent donor base is the source of sustainability for the costs of the NGO, humanitarian projects, and eventually, maybe ultimately, for at least some of the project outcomes." This being the philosophy, it is not surprising that there was no timeline in place for the expectation of the residents and the community to become self-sustaining.

As a result of a component of the screening process imposed on the potential residents by a procedure developed by the NGO, the residents find themselves in an ongoing cultural conflict with one another. This conflict continues to escalate within the community. One of the housing criteria restricted who and how many people would be permitted to live in the home after it was purchased with sweat-equity hours. The only people authorized to live in the home were immediate family members—based on a Western cultural model of parents and children. In the culture of the beneficiaries, the extended family would be considered immediate family.

The NGO staff considered that in the cultural model as dictated by the beneficiaries it would be too difficult to track who lives at the house and who does not. The NGO thought there would be a probability that too many people living in the home would overrun the capacity of the house. Now there are neighbors watching one another as they individually violate the rules of the NGO and have extended family members stay at the home with them; there is the constant threat of being discovered. This is an ideal area to utilize the process of integrative negotiation so the residents could be encouraged to establish guidelines that are consistent with the social and cultural values of their new community.

The vulnerability of the beneficiaries was evident during the onsite interview when a resident shared,

> "We still go back to the dump during the week and get our goods to sell and come here to see our families on different days. We still need to work; now it is harder to be there, now we walk more and it is harder to get the stuff to our families."

In other cases, the families actually stay away from the house for weeks at a time, as they remain at the city dump to continue to collect saleable goods. This behavior that takes the residents in and out of the community for extended periods has caused conflict among the residents and seems to keep the complexion of the population in a constant state of instability.

Since there is no timeline to determine when the community will become economically self-sustaining, it is doubtful there is sufficient motivation or likelihood that it will occur in the near future. There is also the issue of the definition of *sustainability* and how it will be recognized, if and when it occurs. It would be difficult to predict the economic sustainability of this project and if specific services will continue for future generations. A very impressive component of the project is the attention and proactive measures taken to preserve and restore the environment where the community development project has taken place. This project plan and budget included a unique sustainable waste-water filtration that has been developed for the community by volunteer professional engineers. Reforestation is currently occurring at the project site to restore the trees that had been cut to develop the property for the project; this will have a positive impact on the current residents and future generations.

## Communities' Economic Development with Livestock

*Program Objective:*

To help the residents of a poor village that was significantly damaged by a hurricane with community economic development through housing and livestock.

*Project Description:*

The goal was to assist the residents in lifting themselves from impoverished conditions to a level of sustainable economic growth. This village is wedged between the ocean and mountains and is surrounded by cattle ranches. Most of the 2,000 people living in the village are property owners who hold a title to their very small plot of land and live in humble dwellings with dirt floors. Prior to the hurricane, this village was already struggling to survive and existing in extreme poverty. The hurricane brought considerable damage but also the attention of developed countries to some of the needs of this neglected population, and then new resources became available. The average family has approximately eight people living in the same home. Many of the men from the village work on the surrounding cattle ranches for very low wages (below a dollar a day), and the families are unable to support the educational expenses of their children to attend the distant public schools. Nor was there enough money to meet basic needs of food and shelter. Medical evaluations conducted by the NGO staff determined that the entire population suffered from dehydration and malnutrition and only had occasional access to medical care when medical personnel visited, so they had no attention for extended periods of time.

The project manager has shared the following information. The Elders of the community had heard word about this particular foundation/NGO and their ability to assist in the economic development for impoverished communities. The residents of the community had identified the problem and had potential solutions to propose—possible if they were given the appropriate resources. The NGO program manager was approached by the elders of the community and, after a four-hour walk to the organization's office, they requested help to support their own communal development initiatives. The elders of the village proposed that the NGO lend them enough capital and resources to begin a cattle ranch. They were willing to build enclosed areas, raise the cattle, use some meat for their own benefit, and sell the surplus at the market. None of the residents had previous experience or training in business skills. This project was being proposed in a geographic area outside the limits of where the NGO usually conducted projects, but they were aware of additional excess funding made available to the country after the hurricane damage and agreed to apply for the funds on behalf of the community. They also agreed to manage the project.

Using the project-cycle model, the beneficiaries had requested assistance at the first stage of the project cycle with the problem identified, the possible solutions (concept/idea), and alternatives to the proposed solutions, and they are beginning the process of integrative negotiation with the NGO of their choice.

During the onsite project interviews, the elders shared that many alternatives to the cattle ranch were investigated. The NGO staff approached the neighboring cattle communities with the elders to help determine the positive and negative impact of a startup cattle ranch in the area. These communities were also considered stakeholders in the negotiation. Their interest was apparent on two levels: the new startup would create more competition, and the existing cattle ranchers already employed the people interested in starting up the business and it would be very difficult to replace them considering the location of the ranches and the wages they were paying. The existing cattle ranchers were opposed to the start-up of a competitive business and were fearful the NGO would provide resources that were not currently available to them, giving the new business an advantage over the existing businesses.

The project manager shared,

> "I helped facilitate those meetings, and it was difficult for everyone, because the cattle ranchers did not want to lose their help (the men from the village), and they did not want more competition in the cattle industry; but the villagers were feeling like slaves to them, working so cheap for so long. In the past when the village men would ask for more money they were denied immediately. When we showed up with the men from the village and spoke of the possibility of investing in cattle for the village, the ranchers mocked and jeered at the village men and made jokes about their ability to run a business. The village men did not want to continue or cooperate with any discussions and just wanted us to give them the funding and they would start the ranch on their own. Very soon they had to learn this would not be possible."

At the time of the research, the project was at the beginning phases and it was an exciting time in the village. New wells were being drilled so there would be an adequate supply of water for the residents and the expected livestock. The NGO staff and elders had negotiated a slightly higher wage for the cattle ranch workers to stay on the jobs for an extended period of time. All interested stakeholders were able to negotiate an alternative solution to economic development for this community. The

NGO would provide capital to help the women of the village raise piglets as a means of elevating the collective community income. The community agreed that the first beneficiaries of the additional economic resource would be the children, as the parents would then afford their educational costs.

*Project Analysis:*

This project does have the components necessary to build an economically sustainable community. One of the significant advantages of this project is that the beneficiaries of the resources have lived together in a village community for many generations; they have an established hierarchy of leadership through elders who are able to represent the voice of the people. This is a strong foundation from which to build because this community has been making collective decisions and collaborating for many generations. Also, the beneficiaries of this project are landowners and already have a personal and historic investment in the property that will be developed.

This will be an interesting project to observe in the future to determine if the village does indeed become economically self-sustaining; it has begun with the key ingredients and a strong foundation.

## Education Sponsorship as a Bridge to Sustainable Economic Development

*Program Objective:*

Educate impoverished children to give them the opportunity to become economically self-sustaining in the future.

*Project Description:*

This is an educational sponsorship program for impoverished children living at or near a large suburban city dump. They are not able to attend the local public schools because their families cannot afford the $100 cost of uniforms, books, and school supplies, and indeed, also depend on these children to help the family by gathering food and searching for recyclable items at the city dump. The project's declared objective is to sponsor the academic education of needy children and to provide additional benefits to their families. There is a much greater need for the funding of educational sponsorships than there are resources available for the families requesting assistance.

*NGO:*

In essence, the NGO has agreed to pay the public-school fees for the children and to provide a structured after-school program for additional academic and social support; and in exchange, the family must agree to keep the children in school and off the dump after school. This a predetermined agreement stated by the NGO and those specific terms are not negotiable. The NGO does provide other integrated services accompanied with the educational assistance: if a child is sponsored for educational benefits, the entire family then becomes affiliated with the NGO and is eligible for resources provided by the NGO—e.g., general medical and dental care, assistance obtaining gainful employment, food, and housing, etc. The long-term goal of this organization is that children will get the education that is required to one day become economically self-sustaining members of the community.

*Beneficiaries:*

The process to determine eligibility begins when a family member, either the child or an adult, approaches the NGO and makes a request for services. A local social worker then performs a structured assessment of the family's needs and advocates for additional services, if appropriate, at weekly staff meetings as resources become available to the NGO. Each family that has a child with perfect attendance at school for the week will be given supplemental food to help maintain the family, since the child will not be available to contribute labor on behalf of the family at the dump.

*Donors:*

The NGO does maintain an unusually loyal and consistent donor base that makes generous contributions in financial, social, and human capital, but none of the projects are sustainable without the NGO. Unless the beneficiaries of the projects are able to maintain the same resources without the NGO, the beneficiaries will forever be dependent on the NGO, just as the operating costs of the NGO are dependent on the donors. These projects are not self-sustaining in the traditional definition as given by the United Nations. Only according to the unique definition assigned by the organization itself are they able to call themselves self-sustaining.

*Project Analysis:*

This NGO has been providing educational sponsorships and other integrated services in excess of fifteen years to impoverished populations in underdeveloped countries. The funding of administrative costs of the NGO, along with all services for the beneficiaries, is provided through donors. During the onsite interview, the project manager was asked if this is considered a successful/sustainable project and he stated,

*"Yes, this organization and its projects survive on donor dollars and are sustainable because our donors are diverse in nature and have a long-time history of supporting these projects."*

This organization endorses the concept that due to long-term relationships with their loyal donors, as demonstrated through consistent contributions, the NGO itself is sustainable through an endowment fund, as are the projects. The NGO is hopeful that they are providing services that will empower the beneficiaries to one day become self-sustaining. They do not have a formal project evaluation process, but give examples of many families that have become economically independent as a result of the resources developed into programs delivered by this NGO.

This NGO hosts approximately 120 volunteers a year and maintains an operating budget of more than three million dollars with annual growth. The families that take part in this program for the education of their children have become a community among themselves. They have learned that they have a common goal and value the education of their children. They have collaborated and cooperated to increase the benefits of the program, and they have collectively reaped the rewards of systematically resolving conflict within their self-made community. These are people that most probably would not have met one another had they not had their children in this program and they developed a community around a common goal.

Integrative negotiation is a process that is an essential element in the various programs provided by this NGO, and it is at the heart of the organization along with educational sponsorships. Although the conditions of eligibility for educational sponsorship are not negotiable, all elements of the integrative services for the beneficiaries are negotiated with each family.

If a family would like to take advantage of the medical care—such as vaccinations for the children, or dental care—or if they want a new cooking stove or new cooking utensils, they negotiate for an amount of time they will give back to the NGO in terms of labor in exchange for the service or product. Oftentimes the labor that is contributed will be a contract to help another beneficiary build a house, or child care, or cleaning, or helping to plant and maintain a garden.

One of the beneficiaries reported in the interview that he had learned carpentry from a volunteer during his "pay-back hours" helping another resident, and now he is able to support his family using those skills. This NGO has a large area of land where the administrative buildings and medical support staff have offices. One of the beneficiaries of the program reported that rather than go to the dump for resources, she has volunteered hours cleaning the area in exchange for food for her family. When the researcher interviewed her, she showed such pride in her work and effort that provided benefits for her family; with a big smile, she showed all the areas she had completed cleaning. This project is an example of the unintended consequences of humanitarian aid having a positive result. Indeed, for the most part the resources made available to the beneficiaries are driven by the identification of need as identified and asserted by the beneficiaries.

# Microloan Urban Style

*Project Objective:*

To assist women in becoming economically self-sustaining through the systematic disbursement of microloans that provides capital for a micro-enterprise.

*Project Description:*

The NGO provides a small amount of financial capital to individual women or small groups of women to support a micro-enterprise within the urban area where they currently live. The capital is provided in the form of a loan, and borrowers are charged an interest rate that is to be repaid within a specific time frame; all members of the group, as a collective, are held responsible for each individual loan. The microloans generally occur as part of a loan cycle; when one loan is repaid in a timely manner and the business demonstrates adequate success, a new loan cycle begins, and the women can use the funds to reinvest and grow their businesses. The average loan per person is $40–$150 (U.S.) per loan cycle; each enterprise experiences approximately nine loan cycles prior to becoming self-sustaining. The NGO also provides informal educational meetings designed to teach the women basic accounting, money management, and business skills.

After the weekly loan payment is made on behalf of the group, the women are able to spend the profits from the businesses on their own priorities.

*Beneficiaries:*

This program is located in an urban area inside a large city in an underdeveloped country in Central America; the residents live in extreme poverty, are homeless, most likely have very limited formal education if any, and may be carrying a baby on their back with more children alongside them. They have only the goods that they can beg for or get from the city streets, and they have no resources or means to rise above their current living circumstance.

It can be realistically anticipated that this project is benefiting the current generation and will have a positive impact on future generations through income generated for the education of children, better nutrition, medical intervention, and health education. The project manager stated that, as part of the negotiated agreement, each enterprise is evaluated as to the long-term impact on the environment. The expectation is that there will be minimal negative impact on the environment on both a long- and short-term basis, therefore the projects can be maintained within the current ecosystem.

*Donors:*

This NGO attracts multiple, loyal, long-term and varied donors. Many of these donors philosophically consider their donation an investment that contributes to the collective good of the world by supporting entrepreneurship around the world.

*Project Analysis:*

The NGO's administrative costs continue to be dependent on acquiring operating capital from individual donors. One of the major differences between this NGO and many others is that it has developed a strategic plan that intends not only for the borrowers to become economically self-sustaining, but for the operating of the NGO to become economically self-sustaining. The interest from the loans contributes to the cost of operation of the NGO, and eventually, as the number of loans increases, the current dependence of the NGO and the beneficiaries on individual donation will decrease.

All stages of the project cycle are negotiated on an individual or group basis. The concept for the enterprise must first be initiated by the woman; then the plan—including a budget, how the project will be implemented, and how the project will be evaluated for success—is further negotiated with a representative of the NGO. The primary stakeholders in the negotiation process are the representatives of the NGO, the individual loan recipient, and the entire recipient group.

The NGO requires that each woman or group of women develop a business plan with the assistance of a local social worker.

This is a local person, usually trained by the NGO, who teaches the women basic accounting skills. The business plan is then presented. It may be presented by the potential borrower or by a group of women to the NGO. It may be presented by an individual woman to an existing group of women that is a recipient of loans from the NGO. Terms of the repayment of the loan are then negotiated either directly with the NGO by the individual, or with the existing group of women responsible for the loans.

The project manager, who is a local woman, shared her understanding that the very nature of the microloan industry philosophy in the philanthropic world is to empower the borrower to become independent and financially sustainable. The interviewee stated that the best method of ensuring the sustainability of the project is to require the borrower to assume the responsibility, rights, and power of a major stakeholder on the negotiation of a microloan.

This project has empirically demonstrated the strong correlation between negotiation with the beneficiaries at the idea/concept stage and the sustainability of a project. The group of women borrows the capital, and the members are collectively responsible for the repayment. Becoming economically self-sustaining, they remain a business and social network for one another.

## Microloan with Extended Services

*Project Objective:*

To assist women in becoming economically self-sustaining through the system of microcredit with extended services.

*Project Description:*

This project began in 1998 with twenty-eight microloans. Since early 2006, approximately 5,000+ rural women were receiving micro-credit loans with a staff of twenty indigenous loan officers. The loans are given to small groups of women (four to six members) for individual development of enterprise. The entire small group of women is responsible for the repayment of the loan in a timely manner with interest. If one woman falls into default on her repayment of the loan, it behooves the group to make payments on her behalf because a non-payment would reflect poorly on the group and carry the consequence of the inability to obtain future loans.

This is a traditional microloan program with the exception of the offering of the nonfinancial services, or extended services, to each family. All loan members in good standing (i.e., loans are current in repayment) are eligible for medical care for the family, and children receive educational sponsorships. All loan recipients must negotiate time and funds for the education of their children; the amount of money provided by the NGO is usually given on a sliding scale depending on the money the new entrepreneur is able to generate at the time. The biweekly repayment meetings serve several purposes: The women take the time from their businesses to meet and support one another, and the groups receive informal education on the topic of their choice. The indigenous local loan officer receives training in several topics, and she later presents and facilitates educational meetings for the borrowers. The loan officer shared with the researcher that this has been an effective means of spreading information about the community, often enabling people to learn about health and nutrition. The borrowers sharing the information are increasing their social capital in the community and are being sought out for the information of the week.

Another extended benefit to the micro-lending borrowers is the provision of medical care and/or educational sponsorship for the children; this too is negotiated with each individual recipient and based on family need. Local loan officers facilitate the educational programs, building leadership skills and social capital within communities—another step in ensuring the maintenance of the program, borrowing group, as well as the economic sustainability of the individual.

*Beneficiaries:*

The identified population for this project is impoverished women in a rural area of an underdeveloped country. Thousands of women with children living in this geographic region have been widowed following thirty years of civil war; they have no economic means for survival and are unable to afford the school fees for the education of their children. There are high incidences of malnutrition among the population, poor access to potable water, and vulnerability to many illnesses that have elevated the rate of premature deaths in the area.

*Project Analysis:*

This NGO reports a 98 percent success rate of loan repayment and observes various levels of self-sustainability for the borrowers. The local project manager for the organization attributes a large portion of their success to the system of integrative services; this is further supported by the interviews with the beneficiaries and observed in the field through the voluntary attendance at the educational meetings. The researcher observed several of these educational meetings and the women seemed to hunger for the education and general information, asking many questions throughout the discussion.

This NGO understands and demonstrates the correlation between negotiation and sustainability for both themselves and their clients. The client is involved with every stage of the project management cycle; starting at the idea/concept stage, she has been acknowledged as a major stakeholder. Education has been provided to the beneficiaries, and therefore the beneficiaries have been empowered to make informed decisions regarding their lives and those of their families.

# REFERENCES

"Appreciative Inquiry." http://www.new-paradigm.co.uk/ Apprecia tive.htm.

Appreciative Inquiry Commons. Case Western Reserve University. http://appreciativeinquiry.case.edu/intro/whatisai.cfm.

Babbie, E. 2001. *The Practice of Social Research 9th ed*. Belmont, CA: Wadsworth/Thompson Learning.

Background http://www.new-paradigm.co.uk/Appreciative.htm.

Barbier, E. B. 1987. "The concept of sustainable development," *Environmental Conservation*. 14(2) 101-110.

Basserman, M. H., T. Magliozzi, and M. A. Neale. 1985. "Integrative Bargaining in a Competitive Market," *Organizational Behavior & Human Decision Processes*. 35 (3), pp. 294-313.

Berg, B. L. 2004. *Qualitative Research Methods for the Social Sciences (5th ed.)*. Cambridge, MA: Pearson.

Breslin, J. W., and J. Z. Rubin. 1999. *Negotiation Theory and Practice*. Cambridge, MA: Program on Negotiation at Harvard Law School.

Briggs, C. L. 1986. *Learning How to Ask: A Sociolinguistic Appraisal of the Role of the Interview in Social Science Research*. New York: Cambridge University Press.

Brundtland Commission Report. 1987. *Our Common Future*. Oxford: World Commission on Environment and Development. United Nations http://www. un.org/esa/sustdev/csd/ policy. htm.

Bryman, A. 2001. *Social Research Methods*. New York: Oxford University Press. pp. 90-91.

Case Western Reserve University's Weatherhead School of Management http://www.appreciativeinquiry.case.edu/

Chiseri-Strater, and E., Stone-Sunstein, B. 1997. *Fieldworking: Reading and Writing Research*. Upper Saddle River, N.J. USA: Blair Press.

Cohen, D. and L. Prusak. 2001. *In Good Company: How Social Capital*

*Makes Organizations.* Cambridge, MA: Harvard Business School.

Constantino, C. and Merchant, A. 1996. *Designing Conflict Management Systems.* San Francisco, CA: Jossey-Bass.

Cosier, R. A. and T. L. Ruble. 1981. "Research on Conflict Handling Behavior; An Experimental Approach," *Academy of Management Journal.* 24 (4) pp. 816-831.

Creswell, J. W. 1998. *Qualitative Inquiry and Research Design, Choosing Among Five Traditions.* Thousand Oaks, CA: Sage Publications, Inc.

Diener, E. and Crandall, R. 1978. *Social Research Methods.*

Dinsmore, P. C. and Cooke-Davis, T.J. 2005. *The Right Projects Done Right.*

Dos Santos, T. 1971. "The Structure of Dependence," in K.T. Fann and Hodges, D.C., eds. *Readings in U. S. Imperialism.* Boston: Porter Sargent, p.226.

Easterly, W. 2006. *The White Man's Burden: Why the West's Efforts to Aid the Rest Have Done So Much Ill and So Little Good.* New York, NY: Penguin Press.

Easterly, W. 2004. "Why Doesn't Aid Work?" *Essay for Cato Unbound.*

Eaton, S.E., "Appreciative Inquiry: An Overview" http://www.scribd.com/doc/56010589/Appreciative-Inquiry-An-Overview"

Eppen, G., Gould, F.J., Schmidt, C. 1994. *Introductory Management Science (4th ed.).* New York: Prentice Hall.

Ertel, D. 1999. "Turning Negotiation into a Corporate Capacity," *Negotiation.* Cambridge, MA: Harvard Business School Press.

Escobar, A., 1995. *Encountering Development, the Making and Unmaking of the Third World.* Princeton: Princeton University Press.

Fischer, F. 1995. *Evaluating Public Policy.* Chicago, IL: Nelson-Hall.

Fisher, R., and W. Ury. 1991. *Getting to YES, Negotiating Agreement Without Giving In.* New York: Penguin Books.

Folsberg, K., Mooz, H., and Cotterman. 2005. *Visualizing Project Management: Models and Frameworks for Mastering Complex Systems, 3 ed.:* New York, NY: John Wiley & Sons.

Francis, D. 2002. *People, Peace, and Power: Conflict Transformation in Action.* London; Sterling, VA: Pluto Press.

Frank, A. G. 1993. *ReOrient World System History.* Berkeley, CA: University of CA Press.

Frisbie, D. A. 1999. "Estimating Reliability Under Generalizability Theory Model for Test Scores Composed of Testlets," *Applied Measurements in Education,* Vol. 12, No.3, pp. 237-255.

Fulton, K. 2006. *Looking Out for the Future, An Orientation for Twenty-first Century Philanthropists.* Global Business Network.

Galjart, B. F. 1996. "Sustainability as the maintenance of things: analogies for an environmental sociology," *Innovations,* 9 (4): pp. 477-89.

Gruenwald, G.. 1999. *The Dangers and Inconsistencies of Normative Approaches to Humanitarian Aid.* http:// www.projectqualite.org.

Holsti, O.R. 1969. *Content Analysis for the Social Sciences and Humanities.* Reading, MA: Addison-Wesley.

Howes, N. R. 2001. *Modern Project Management: Successfully Integrating Project Management Knowledge Areas.* AMACOM: New York: American Management Association.

Hoyle, R. H., Harris, M.J., and Judd, C.M. 2002. *Research Methods in social Relations (7th ed.).* USA: Wadsworth.

http://appreciativeinquiry.case.edu/join/easySubmit.cfm.

http://www.mt-online.com/component/content/article/77-february2007/228-building-strength-based-organizations.html.

http://www.positivechange.org/downloads/AI_and_Spiritual_ResonanceV.Final.pdf .

Huberman, A. M. and Miles, B. M. 1994. "Data Management and Analysis Methods," *Handbook of Qualitative Research* edited by Denzin & Lincoln. Thousand Oaks, CA: Sage. pp. 428-44.

Jäger, Urs. 2010. *Managing Social Businesses. Mission, Governance, Strategy and Accountability.*

Khator, R. 1998. "The new paradigm: From development administration to sustainable development," *International Journal of Public Administration.* 21(12), pp. 1777-1801.

Kinni, T. "The Art of Appreciative Inquiry," *The Harvard Business School Working Knowledge for Business Leaders Newsletter,* September 22, 2003.

Le Compte, M., Preissle., D.J. 1993. *Ethnography and Qualitative Design in Educational Research (2nd ed.).* San Diego, CA: Academic Press.

Leedy, P. D. and Ormrod, J.E. 2005. *Practical Research Planning and Design (8th.ed.).* Columbus, OH: Pearson.

Letts, C. W., Ryan W. and Grossman, A. 1997. "Venture Capital: What Foundations Can Learn from Venture Capitalists," *Harvard Business Review.*

Lewicki, R. J., Saunders, D., Minton, B. 2003. *Negotiation 4th ed.:* New York, NY: McGraw Hill.

Levy. 1984. "Multivariate Decision Making," *Journal of Economic Theory.* Feb.

Lueptow, Mueller, Hammes and Master. 1977. *Social Methods Research.* "The impact of informed consent regulations on response rate and response bias."

Martin, D., J., Mayfield, M., Mayfield, P. and Herbig. 1998. "International Negotiations: An Entirely Different Animal," *Journal of Professional Marketing Services.* Binghamton, NY. pp. 43-61.

Maxwell, J. A. 2005. *Qualitative Research Design An interactive Approach (2nd ed.).* Thousand Oaks, CA: Sage.

McCann, G., McCloskey. 2003. *From the Local to the Global: Key Issues in Development Studies.* London; Sterling, VA: Pluto Press.

Middleton, N., O'Keefe, P., Visser, R.. 2001. *Negotiating Poverty: New Directions, Renewed Debate.* London: Sterling, VA: Pluto Press.

Miles, M. B. and Huberman, A. M. 1994. *Qualitative Data Analysis: An expanded source book. (2nd ed.).* Thousand Oaks, CA: Sage.

Nachmias, C. H. and Nachmias, D. 2002. *Research Methods in Social Sciences (6th ed.).* New York: Worth Publishing.

Nierenberg, G. 1973. *Fundamentals of Negotiating.* New York: Hawthorne.

Nightingale and Cromby. 1999. *Social Constructionist Psychology.* Buckingham: Open University Press.

Ophuls, W., Boyan, S. Jr. 1992. *Ecology and Politics of Scarcity Revisited: The Unraveling of the American Dream.* New York: W.H. Freeman.

Panayiotopoulos, Prodromos, Capps, Gaviv. 2001. *World Development: An Introduction.* London; Sterling, VA.

Parfitt, and Trevor. 2002. *The End of Development: Modernity, Post-Modernity and Development.* London; Sterling, VA: Pluto Press.

Patton, M. Q. 1990. *Qualitative Evaluation and Research Methods.* (2nd ed.). Newbury Park, CA: Sage.

Porter, M.E., Kramer, M.R. (1999). *Philanthropy's New Agenda: Creating Value.* Harvard Business Review.

Prahatad, C.K., Hammond, A. (2002). *Serving the World's Poor, Profitably.* Harvard Business Review. Harvard Press.

Raiffa, H. 1982. *Art and Science of Negotiation.* Cambridge, MA: Harvard University Press.

Raiffa, H., J. Richardson and D. Metcalfe. 2002. *Negotiation Analysis: The Science and Art of Collaborative Decision Making.* Belknap Press of Harvard University.

Rankin. 2002. *Feminist Economics. Social capital, microfinance and the politics of development:* pp.1-24.

Rossi, P. H., Freeman, H.E., and Lipsey, M.W. 1991. *Evaluation A*

*Systematic Approach* (6th ed.). Thousand Oaks, CA: Sage.

Rostow, W. 1971. *The Stages of Economic Growth*. Cambridge, MA: Cambridge University Press.

Rowe, M. 2008. *Micro-Affirmations and Micro-inequities in the Journal of the International Ombudsman Association, Volume 1, Number 1, March 2008*.

Sachs, J. 2005. *The End of Poverty: Economic Possibilities for Our Time*. New York, NY: The Earth Institute, Columbia University.

Sachs, J. and Fukuda-Parr, S. 2003. "If We Cared to, We Could Defeat World Poverty," *Los Angeles Times*. Los Angeles, CA. July 9, 2003, pg. 13.

Saunders, H. 1981. We Need a Larger Theory of Negotiation: The Importance of Pre-Negotiation Phases. *Negotiation Theory and Practice*.

Schramm, J. B. 2006. "The Business of Giving, A survey of wealth and philanthropy," *The Economist*, February.

"The Science of Happiness," *Time Magazine*. January 17, 2005. http://www.authentichappiness.sas.upenn.edu/images/Time Magazine/Time-Happiness.pdf.

Seale, C. 1999. *The Quality of Qualitative Research*. London: Sage.

Sen, A. K. 1999. *Development as Freedom*. New York: Knopf.

Simons, T. and T. M. Tripp. 2003. "The Negotiation Checklist," *Negotiation, Readings, Exercise and Cases (4th ed.)*. Lewicki, Saunders, Minton, and Barry. New York, NY: McGraw-Hill.

Strepp, J., Sweeney, K.M. and Johnson, R.L. 1998. "Interest-Based Negotiation: An Engine Driving Change," *The Journal for Quality and Participation*. Sept.-Oct.: Cincinnati, OH.

Sudman, S. and Bradburn, N.M. 1982. *Asking Questions 1st* ed.; San Francisco: Jossey-Bass.

Sunkel, O. 1969. "National Development Policy and External Dependence in Latin America," *The Journal of Development Studies*, Vol. 6. October 1969, p. 23.

Trochim, W. M. 2001. *The Research Methods Knowledge Base (2nd ed.)*. Cincinnati, OH: Atomic Dog Publishers.

Turnbull, C. 1972. *Mountain People*. New York: Simon & Schuster.

United Nations Development Report. 2005.http://www.un.org.

United Nations Humanitarian Affairs Report. 2005. http://www.un.org.

United Nations Millennium Development Goals Report. 2005. http://www.un.org.

United Nations, Statistical information. http://www.un.org/esa/sustdev/freshwat.htm.

Ury, W. L. and Brett, J.M., and Goldberg, S.B. 1993. *Getting Disputes Resolved, Designing Systems to Cut the Costs of Conflict.* Cambridge, MA: Program on Negotiation at Harvard Law School.

Warfield, J. 1994. *A Handbook of Interactive Management.*

Webster's II, New College Dictionary. 1999. Boston: Houghton Mifflin Company, 1111.

Weiss, C. H. 1972. *Evaluation Research: Methods of Assessing Program Effectiveness.* Englewood Cliffs, NJ: Prentice Hall.

Whitney, D. and Trosten-Bloom, A. 2003. *The Power of Appreciative Inquiry: a practical guide to positive change.* San Francisco: Berrett-Koehler Publishers, Inc.

Wolfensohn, J. 2004. "The Growing Threat of Global Poverty World Bank," *International Herald Tribune.* Paris. April 24, 2004. pg. 6.

World Bank. 1999. Poverty Net. http:/www.worldbank. org/poverty/scapital

Yin, R. K. 1984. *Case Study Research: Design and Methods.* Beverly Hills, CA: Sage.

Yunus, M. 2010. *Building Social Business: The New Kind of Capitalism That Serves Humanity's Most Pressing Needs.*

Yunus, M. 2008. *Creating a World Without Poverty: Social Business and the Future of Capitalism.*

# INDEX

CPSIA information can be obtained at www.ICGtesting.com
Printed in the USA
LVOW07s0008270814

401118LV00007B/241/P